CHRIS FOLMSBEE

WHAT DID I SIGN UP FOR?

THINGS EVERY YOUTH MINISTRY VOLUNTEER SHOULD KNOW

CHRIS FOLMSBEE

WHAT DID I SIGN UP FOR?

THINGS EVERY YOUTH MINISTRY VOLUNTEER SHOULD KNOW

youth
specialties

ZONDERVAN.com/
AUTHORTRACKER
follow your favorite authors

ZONDERVAN

What Did I Sign Up For?
Copyright © 2011 by Chris Folmsbee

YS Youth Specialties is a trademark of YOUTHWORKS!, INCORPORATED and is registered with the United States Patent and Trademark Office.

Requests for information should be addressed to:

Zondervan, *Grand Rapids, Michigan 49530*

Library of Congress Cataloging-in-Publication Data

Folmsbee, Chris.
    What did I sign up for? / by Chris Folmsbee.
        p.   cm.
    Includes bibliographical references and index.
    ISBN 978-0-310-57900-7 (softcover : alk. paper)
    1. Church work with teenagers. I. Title.
  BV4447.F662 2011
  259'.23—dc23
                                   2011025557

Cover design: SharpSeven Design
Interior design: David Conn

Printed in the United States of America

11 12 13 14 15 16 /DCI/ 23 22 21 20 19 18 17 16 15 14 13 12 11 10 9 8 7 6 5 4 3 2 1

CONTENTS

ACKNOWLEDGMENTS

As with every book I write, there are many people to thank for their contributions toward making it as helpful as possible to youth workers. First I need to thank the countless volunteer youth workers who've served teens and their families beside me all these years. Your passion and commitment is inspiring. Second, a big thanks to Tony Myles—an Ohio senior pastor with many years of youth ministry experience. His contributions to this book are too numerous to even begin pointing out. The sidebars, many of the stories, and a fair amount of the content can be attributed to Tony and his thinking and writing. This isn't the first time Tony has helped me make a project great, and I hope it isn't the last. Third, I'd like to thank Mike Wonch—former youth pastor, volunteer in his church, and now an editor. His creative, editorial contributions to this book were most helpful and appreciated. Fourth, I thank Jason Sivewright for his fine work on the videos on the DVD that accompanies this book. Finally, I want to thank my wife Gina and my three kids, Megan, Drew, and Luke, for their ongoing love, friendship, and encouragement.

PART ONE

FOUNDATIONS OF YOUTH MINISTRY I: THEOLOGY, PHILOSOPHY, AND SOCIOLOGY

CHAPTER 1

UNDERSTANDING YOUTH MINISTRY

I didn't grow up with a youth pastor at my church; instead, aside from the sporadic random adult pitching in when desperately needed, the youth ministry was led primarily by two volunteers—a husband-and-wife team, Tom and Karen. Tom was a cabinetmaker, and Karen was a schoolteacher. Together they taught our youth Sunday school class and on occasion led a youth group outing to the park, a sporting event, or a concert.

At times we were absolutely horrible to Tom and Karen. There weren't many of us in the group (maybe 12 on a really crowded night); but whoever attended an activity usually made life for Tom and Karen more difficult than it needed to be. We often were rude, obnoxious, mischievous, and at times just plain punks. I assume our strategy was to get them mad enough that they'd quit being our youth group leaders, and we could stop going to Sunday school and other youth group activities.

When I reflect upon some of the things we did and said to them, I'm embarrassed. In truth, we didn't dislike Tom and Karen—we just hated getting up to go to church and usually took it out on them.

Tom and Karen were very generous people. They didn't have much, but what they did have they shared willingly with us. Occasionally Tom and Karen would sacrifice and buy food for our group or even gifts on our birthdays and at Christmas. I often wondered why they cared so much. I remember thinking, *Who in their right mind would ever put up with us—and on top of that, still give us gifts?*

I'm not sure if Tom remembers this, but one Sunday morning I was the only one who showed up to Sunday school class. Tom taught the lesson in a very relaxed way for just the two of us, and then we just sat and talked for a while. During our conversation I asked Tom, "Why do you do this? Why do you spend time with us when you could be home, or with your friends, or out to breakfast with your wife, or sleeping in, or whatever else? Why would anyone take what we dish out?"

Tom's response was quiet and pointed. He said, very simply, something to this effect: "I want you to fall so in love with Jesus and live a life so full of his love that it can't help but spill out onto others. I want you, and all the others, to be transformed. I want all of you to experience God in deep and meaningful ways."

Tom understood youth ministry—and at that precise moment, so did I. That's the moment I first felt God's nudge to pursue full-time vocational ministry. Although I haven't seen Tom and Karen since my college graduation (they're pastors now to a wonderful church family and community in North Carolina), they remain an important part of my journey into and through youth ministry.

WHAT IS YOUTH MINISTRY REALLY ALL ABOUT?

Youth ministry is about a lot of things—but of course you know that. I don't have to tell you how many different aspects of life and faith make up what we refer to today as modern-day youth ministry. You are most likely living a cosmic assortment of them in your everyday ministry with teens in your church and community.

Youth ministry is about fun and fellowship. It's about planning trips, teaching classes, celebrating graduations, and attending games, plays, and band concerts, all to live out your love for teens and their families. Youth ministry is about one-on-one discipleship, facilitating small groups, and finding time as often as you can for a space in which your entire group can come together for Scripture, song, and discussion. The list goes on and on and on.

But to me, one aspect stands out…

YOUTH MINISTRY IS ABOUT TRANSFORMATION

A few years ago a youth worker magazine asked me to participate in a panel conversation with a few of my peers. Each of us was to define transformational youth ministry. Here is what I came up with:

At its core, transformational youth ministry is the on-going, holistic process of guiding students toward becoming like Jesus. It is a process of shepherding students through a journey of the spiritual life that fundamentally begins with a shepherd-student relationship, progresses with and through shared spiritual discovery and growth and ends only when the shepherd-student relationship ceases to remain.[1]

Youth ministry is about more than mere change; youth ministry is about transformation. Change is what we know will happen. Change is inevitable. The teens in your church and community can't help but change. Their bodies change, their minds change, their hobbies and interests change, their relationship webs change, their career plans change. Change just happens.

Transformation, on the other hand, can't happen without you and other adults in your church (yielded to the Holy Spirit) pointing teens toward Jesus' life and ministry as a model for life. Transformation is what we pray for, expect, and hope will happen. That is the very reason we do youth ministry.

TRANSFORMATIONAL YOUTH MINISTRY IS ONGOING

One of the chief characteristics of transformational youth ministry is that it's ongoing—it evolves without interruption. Transformational youth ministry endures through all the changes in teens' lives to remain as a (if not the only) consistent factor in their always-changing lives. This doesn't mean that the teens in your group see what you do as ongoing; you, however, *must*. Transformational youth ministry evolves without interruption so that your teens have something biblically consistent in their lives. It continues so that relationships can flourish. It never ceases so that practices can be developed and environments cultivated in which adolescents can live out Jesus' teachings and deeds. Transformational youth ministry continues so that the teens in your group have a community where they can be real. Transformational youth ministry is never static, but it continuously evolves as the Holy Spirit leads.

About a month or so ago I bumped into Sarah, a former youth group member. She's married now and has two beautiful children. We were passing each other in a local store, realized we knew each other, and then spent about 20 minutes catching up. During our conversation Sarah asked if I was still involved in youth work.

---

1. Chris Folmsbee, "Transformers: Ministry That Changes Lives," *Network Magazine*, Fall 2007.

"I will always be involved in youth work in one way, shape, or form," I replied. "It isn't my job anymore, but I still hang out with kids almost every week."

Sarah said, "One of the reasons I always came to everything that we did in church was because I knew you and the others cared. I couldn't always count on that at home or at school or even at work. I always knew that it was more than just fun and games for you all. I could always tell that you really cared about us. Thanks."

Transformational youth ministry evolves without interruption for many reasons. For people like Sarah, transformational youth ministry still moves in her life—a stabilizing place to get the bearings of a life of faith.

TRANSFORMATIONAL YOUTH MINISTRY IS HOLISTIC

A few years ago I was on a mission trip with about 75 middle schoolers. There were about a dozen of us adult leaders guiding them as we served the homeless people of Nashville. I was driving one of the vans. My van was full of guys. (Been there, haven't you?) You know what that van smelled like after a week of sweaty middle school guys ate in it, slept in it, and did many other things in it.

At one point the smell in the van was too much to tolerate any longer. I called the other van drivers and told them to meet me at a particular store at the next exit. I marched these 12 guys into this store. I took them right to the deodorant aisle and said, "Gentlemen, this is the deodorant aisle. Deodorant is a substance to disguise the way you really smell. Pick one and use it like so."

Transformational youth ministry is concerned with all aspects of teens' lives, not just with faith or salvation. We also do youth ministry to help guide the whole person. We do youth ministry to help teens grow and develop intellectually, socially, physically, emotionally, and spiritually. Transformational youth ministry sees the whole teen and doesn't compartmentalize, speaking only into preferred "parts." The honest truth is: *Your youth ministry has an opportunity that few organizations have—to shape teenagers' entire lives*. So we can't focus merely on the spiritual; in addition we must continue to discover how the gospel reaches into every area of life.

Don't get me wrong. Teens must surrender their lives to Jesus and choose to follow him with their whole hearts, minds, souls, and strength and learn how to love others as themselves. However, we must also guide them toward knowing how to do all of that in all of life so that, as they mature beyond their teenage years, they have context for living in the way of Jesus in the midst of real life.

Our youth ministries don't make widgets. We don't spend our days standing in an assembly line spitting out scads of cookie-cutter product. Thank God for that! How uninteresting and ineffective would youth ministry be if we didn't take into consideration the unique characteristics of each one of the teens in our groups? One of the best parts about youth ministry is that we get to serve teens who don't look or behave exactly like one another. (Now, it'd make youth ministry easier if they did look or act the same—assuming *appropriately* was the benchmark.)

Transformational youth ministry takes into consideration the uniqueness of each of our teens and doesn't view them as one kind of person we've constructed to fit our collective ideal. Instead, we're a patient, faithful people awaiting the work of the Holy Spirit in the lives of our teens rather than forcing them to be who we so desperately want them to be—even if who we want them to be is best.

TRANSFORMATIONAL YOUTH MINISTRY IS A PROCESS

A week ago I was invited to a church near Baltimore to do some consulting with their youth ministry. This particular church has a long history of what they call "successful" youth ministry. I was a bit surprised to be invited in the first place. When I arrived I was even more surprised. The walls of the conference room in which we were meeting were filled with sheets of large paper. Listed on each piece of paper was a different aspect of discipleship—terms such as *Word, prayer, service, justice, worship,* etc. Obviously great words and key aspects to our Christian formation. However, leading into each of these wonderful words was the phrase, "Before our students graduate, they will be people of…"

After reviewing each word with me and casting their complete vision for their youth ministry discipleship strategy, the church officials asked me, "Well, what do you think we can do better?" I responded with a question of my own: "Well, what if a student of yours doesn't possess all of those traits before she graduates? Does that mean you've failed? Does that mean the student isn't a follower of Jesus? Just what does that mean?" I continued by asking another question, "What if the students don't care until later in life, or what if it takes them much longer to grow into these traits? Are you still doing effective youth ministry?"

To my surprise I heard a resounding "no" from most of the group. One person, however, said what I was hoping someone would say: "Maybe it isn't so much about what we try to make them into as much as it's about their process of discovering

God? What if we saw our youth ministry more as a place to get teens on their way rather than a finish line?"

Transformational youth ministry makes room for teens to be in *process*. We can't make teens do or be anything they don't want to be. In fact, when we push students to live a particular way without context, meaning, and their own passion, we don't create people equipped for the journey of following Jesus for life; rather we likely create individuals who put on false selves so they don't make us feel unsuccessful.

TRANSFORMATIONAL YOUTH MINISTRY IS ABOUT GUIDING

If transformational youth ministry is about the process more than making products, then it makes sense that it's also about guiding. It isn't about telling a teen "what to do"; it's about showing a teen "how to do."

Sometimes I'm afraid of the fact that many youth workers, paid and volunteer, don't understand the importance of seeing themselves as guides. Have you ever been on an organized backpacking trip? Ever walked through museum with an expert leading the way? Have you ever been on a tour of a factory, a ballpark, or a city? Guides lead—and as they do, they point us in helpful and trusted directions. They don't leave people to tour on their own, lost on the journey, scratching their heads and circled around a map they don't understand. No, guides want those on the tour to take it all in without other distractions. They want to make sure that the tourists or travelers or backpackers experience everything in the fullest possible way.

Transformational youth ministry is like this. We want to guide students toward becoming like Jesus.

But does a guide just give you a map and say, "Good luck?" A bad guide maybe. Or does a good guide stay with you, pointing out the knowledge and information essential for enjoying and benefitting from the experience in the fullest possible way?

In addition, youth ministers who desire to guide students into transformational living don't see themselves as people who direct individuals who are already complete. Instead, transformational youth workers see themselves as directors of unfinished individuals on their way toward becoming more complete. Good guides know it's about the journey and about participation, not merely just disseminating information. (And by the way, this obviously means we must travel with youth on their journey and see ourselves as one of the travelers as much as we see ourselves as merely pointing the way.)

TRANSFORMATIONAL YOUTH MINISTRY IS ABOUT JESUS

I'm privileged to interact with hundreds and sometimes thousands of youth workers every year. And it doesn't take me long to realize whether the youth workers I meet are about Jesus…or about something else.

Unfortunately, many aren't really about leading students toward becoming more like Jesus. Instead they're often merely facilitating recreational activities for adolescents. These youth workers don't really see Jesus as the apex of their ministry efforts. Rather they see events and activities as the main construct of their ministry focus.

Fun and social interaction are good things, but we fall short when they're the end goal of our youth ministries. The church is about conversion, conformity to Christ, and community—not just events and other things that take up time on a calendar, regardless of how fun and engaging they may be.

Do the teens in your youth ministry really know Jesus? Do the teens in your group have the context and meaning for who Jesus is and why following him is imperative to God's mission to restore the world to its intended wholeness? Do your teens have a robust understanding of the gospel, salvation, and justice in the way of Jesus? Or do your teens actually just know about a person named Jesus who we pull out of mothballs to discuss at Christmas and Easter?

I'm not trying to be a downer here. But the reality is that many youth ministries don't seek to know Jesus first—or at all. Many youth ministries are nothing more than a community social organization that provides a place for teens to play video games, eat pizza, and interact with their peers. Again, those are good things, but are they transformational as we have described the meaning of the word so far?

In the end, transformational youth ministry is about guiding teens toward becoming more like Jesus. And of course this means that we need to provide social activities, but we can't stop there. We have to move deeper into the process of helping teens find Jesus and follow him and his teachings.

Transformational youth ministry is about opening up new dimensions of the soul for our teens. It's about a square transforming into a cube; a circle transforming into a cylinder. It's about moving into new dimensions of life and faith and helping teens discover and grow into being more like Jesus. This happens through shared spiritual discovery and growth and consists of a developing relationship anchored by our love for God and others.

Change happens, but transformation is what we hope for, pray for, and expect that the Holy Spirit will do when we're faithful to our calling to serve youth and their families. How are you helping to open new dimensions of the soul in your teens? Are you sharing this experience with them, or are you hoping someone else will show them what it means to live, love, and lead in the way of Jesus?

Tom and Karen—my volunteer youth leaders when I was a teen—were amazing people. They knew what it meant to create and sustain a transformational approach to youth ministry. Although we weren't the busiest youth group in town, we were transformational for sure. Because of Tom and Karen's (and other contributing adults') highly relational, patient, forgiving, encouraging, empowering, authentic, and transparent platform of love, I was exposed to what it means to live in the intended ways of God.

Serving teens and their families can be chaotic and messy; however, I'm convinced that your efforts are worth your time, energy, and sacrifice. I'm absolutely convinced that if you (and others who work with you) are faithful and stay committed to a youth ministry anchored by the life and ministry of Jesus, then you can't help but impact the lives of the teens in your church and community.

It won't be easy, and it won't always be fun, but it will be worth every day, hour, minute, and second you give to help squares become cubes and circles become cylinders. Transformational youth ministry requires that we depend on prayer, create learning environments that teach and inspire, engage the entire family, tie our youth ministries into the greater church community, and be faithful to God's mission to restore the world to its intended wholeness. None of this is possible, however, if we don't find ways to open up new dimensions in our own souls. You and I can't give away what we don't own.

CHAPTER 2

UNDERSTANDING CHRISTIAN FORMATION

Christian formation means spiritual growth and development founded upon love for God and for others.

For youth workers like you and me, *Christian formation* also involves the intentional plan or framework we create and maintain that allows teenagers to understand the importance of developing their entire beings—and *it must be enveloped by a transformational approach to youth ministry* (outlined in the previous chapter).

The goal of Christian formation is for every Christian to participate in God's mission to restore the world toward its intended wholeness.

Understanding where Christian formation begins can help us better recognize how God grows authentic faith through transformational youth ministry. The framework I've used for years to help create environments for transformation consists of five dimensions: Revelation, Foundation, Implication, Integration, and Application.

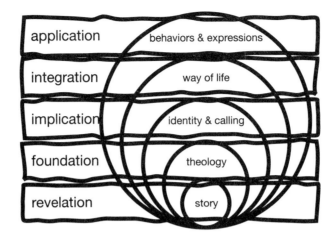

Each of these dimensions helps guide teens toward becoming more like Jesus.

Important note: Keep in mind that each of these five dimensions helps inform, or open up, the others. The illustration appears to display a somewhat phased approach to transformation, but the opposite is actually the case. Because illustrations are one-dimensional, you can't see that teens enter into this process at varying places. In other words, not every teen in your group will begin by understanding formation or discipleship through God's story, the Bible. Neither will all teens in your group integrate a way of life in Jesus once they figure out their identities and callings. Some teens may enter into this process by joining you on a mission trip or other missional experience without even knowing what they've gotten themselves into.

Do you see what I'm suggesting? These dimensions are crucial to the formation process, but they won't necessarily be experienced in a linear fashion. These dimensions will, however, collaborate with one another in order to create opportunities for spiritual transformation.

THE DIMENSION OF REVELATION: ANSWERING THE "WHO IS GOD?" QUESTION

Any study of Scripture will show you that God seldom reveals himself in the same way twice. Even when the waters parted for Joshua as they did for his forerunner Moses, it was less about a new revelation and more about establishing the continuation of leadership. A true revelation from God is just that—*from* God…and on God's terms for the specific person or people with whom God is attempting to communicate. This is why some students love the spiritual pathway that a Bible study or class offers while others crave serving experiences through which they can get their hands dirty. Others desire a connection with the Holy Spirit through worship music; still others prefer a walk in nature.

What's common, though, is that God desires students to discover his already-there presence in their lives and the great story God has invited them to take part in, no matter how that discovery is realized.

The story of God, or the Bible, is God's revelation to us. This dimension is where we begin to understand who God is. Soon it informs the context (or gives meaning) to our theology—opening up the foundation dimension.

THE DIMENSION OF FOUNDATION: ANSWERING THE "WHAT DO I BELIEVE ABOUT GOD?" QUESTION

Experiencing God through God's story, or through another form of revelation, is powerful. It creates a stream of learning that helps teens discover God and begin making deliberate conclusions about their faith.

By helping teens think in terms of the larger story of God, they can better form theological foundations greater than their own experiences and ideas. In other words, one of the wonderful benefits of helping them engage the Bible is that soon the Bible becomes better positioned to live through them.

That's what theology is—a "beyond us" enlargement of our thoughts and convictions about God and Christianity. Theology isn't solely an intellectual pursuit reserved for adults; it's a practical reality for all. There is no age prerequisite for generating context and meaning from the enduring, unfolding narrative of God in our lives that shapes faith into a dynamic dimension of discovery and growth. And the more you help teens form a foundation derived from Scripture, the more they can authentically see God's mission to restore every person around them (including themselves) into God's intended wholeness.

When faith moves from an intellectual pursuit and exercise to a practical reality, it opens up a new dimension—the dimension of implication.

THE DIMENSION OF IMPLICATION: ANSWERING THE "WHO AM I?" AND "WHAT AM I CALLED TO DO?" QUESTIONS

As young people place themselves into the great accounts from Scripture, church history, and present movements locally and globally, their theology becomes more than something they think about; it creates an understanding of identity and calling—both a personal and shared thing. Identity and calling help students to ultimately think in terms of how their presence *now* is a part of something that's been happening since creation—and will culminate with the return of Jesus Christ. This is akin to the difference between a spectator walking on an athletic field versus a player engaging in the contest between the white lines.

When teens know who they are and how their lives uniquely add to the story of God, it creates implications for how they view all of life. It impacts how they think, speak, and act on every level. So, if you truly want students to embrace the implications of their faith from the inside out, then you need to help them see how they're vital parts of God's story and mission. It's also imperative that they see their lives as a means through which to live out the story and mission of God.

When teens become aware of the general and specific callings in their lives, they find meaning in their images and stories. This opens up a new dimension—the dimension of integration.

THE DIMENSION OF INTEGRATION: ANSWERING THE "HOW DO I LIVE?" QUESTION

The most instinctive outflow of teens knowing who they are and what they're called to do is synthesizing all they've come to know and experience. Just as everyone possesses unique ways of waking up and doing life every day, so do we all have unique ways of doing our spiritual lives that create points of integration between who we are at the moment and who we're becoming in the moments to come.

This way of life (or set of virtues) shapes us and is the very impetus for our discovery and growth; in fact, it helps us develop a way or rule of life—a governing-yet-freeing routine that guides how each of us develops internally. We realize and formalize what's important to us and ultimately important to God's mission to restore the world to its intended wholeness.

Developing a way of life—a set of virtues that shapes the way teens live—opens up a new dimension in teens' souls…the dimension of application.

THE DIMENSION OF APPLICATION: ANSWERING THE "HOW DO I PARTICIPATE WITH GOD'S MISSION?" QUESTION

When the dimension of application opens up, teens begin to commit to what I refer to as "missional behaviors and expressions"—outpourings of what's been developed in their hearts through their way of life, their desire to participate with God's mission.

The ways in which teens interact with God, self, and others, and the priorities they seek to live out—essentially the things they do each day to cooperate with God's mission for the sake of the world—encompass this newly developed (or more deeply developed) dimension of the soul.

When teens' behaviors and expressions are formed by their convictions and beliefs, formalized by their growing inner lives, they possess a renewing sense of passion and devotion to God's mission. This dimension of application is where God's story and mission becomes a reality for all those who've yet to encounter God in a personal way. This also is where gospel, culture, and our youth ministries converge.

Transformational youth ministry is about an enduring commitment to Christian formation and opening up new dimensions of the soul. It's about growing closer to Jesus in order to resemble his way of life for the sake of the world.

A youth ministry whose primary focus is transformation can be guided toward cultivating and sustaining an environment for Christian formation—and protecting it for the discovery of new truths about who God is. In other words, a place for students where they can feel free to discover God without feeling as though they're on the "outside looking in" because they haven't yet learned or understood enough.

This protection may come through allowing students to doubt particular truths and ask questions that some might be afraid to ask. A protected environment is incomplete, however, without offering intentional moments of tension to stimulate deeper understanding of faith. Creating tension by not always having an answer or not believing an orthodox view can help teens develop a healthy sense of faith. Their faith becomes more confident because it has been worked out through Scripture, reason, tradition, and experience, not handed down through imposition. One of the worst things we can do to teens is give them simple, cliché answers to hard, pressing questions. Let the tension work for you as you help teens work out their faith. After all, it's *their* faith, not your faith or their parents' faith.

While approaches may vary from one youth worker to another and from one student to another, there are some core values that should guide us as we guide students into deeper levels of spiritual discovery and growth.

CORE VALUE: EXPLORATION

Some teens participate in youth group events and activities because their families require it; others take part simply because their friends are there. Both reasons have their place, but there's simply nothing more influential to spiritual transformation than the freedom to explore God.

Jesus constantly extended invitations to follow him in a variety of ways—some ways highlighted blessings; others highlighted challenges. If you listen well, you can better discern how to challenge a student (and possibly even a family) in a way that creates greater spiritual exploration. Don't let everyone settle for something smaller when there is such a great journey to be taken with God.

CORE VALUE: RESTORATION

All of humanity has been made in the image of God (Genesis 2:2-8). This truth, when understood, runs deep. Each of us, being created in the image of God, is made to resemble God.

Our Christian formation, therefore, is about living into our true image. It's about living into the intentions with which we were created—whole vessels of worship designed to glorify God with all that we are and all that we've yet to become.

Though we've been stained by sin, the stronghold of sin can be overcome through our formation based on Jesus continuously renewing us. Our teens need to know the true image in which they've been created so that they might live into their own story and image, seeking to be continuously renewed.

CORE VALUE: CONVERSION

All believers are called to take hold of their faith and continue to figure out what it means to follow Jesus, but not every believer knows how to do it. That's where you come in—youth workers through their lives must urge teens' ongoing conversion.

It's completely possible for you to allow God's presence in you—and revealed through you—to flood every interaction with your teens. From the things we intentionally say to the powerful seeds our lives instinctively plant, we begin to discern over time how the Holy Spirit is using our conversion to transform teens toward conversions.

CORE VALUE: CONVERSATION

Life isn't meant to be experienced in isolation. Community is a value seen all throughout Scripture. When we help our teens form friendships around the truths of God, those relationships begin producing encouraging fruit.

Teens tend to keep things real and seldom accept slick answers to what they perceive as complex questions. We need to find ways to foster this, for in the end it will create a community where good conversation can occur in every possible direction.

CORE VALUE: PARTICIPATION

Effective youth ministry creates opportunities to develop teens' attitudes and overall ways of thinking. We have to be careful that the programs we lead don't become about our ideas, but about what our teens need. We should use entertaining and culturally appropriate methods, but youth ministry often happens best through whole group participation. If we don't allow our teens the opportunity to join in and contribute in meaningful ways, they will never take steps forward. Youth ministry supports teens' desires for trustworthiness, enabling them to take greater possession of their lives, and for the communities where they live out the mission of God.

CORE VALUE: COLLABORATION

Effective education happens through planned classes, retreats, studies, and activities; it also happens through opportunities that arise spontaneously. Youth workers should look into every human and spiritual resource—from God, who may change your plans at any given point, to students who can offer valuable feedback. Also, don't overlook parents' insights and passions. Church leaders inside and outside your congregation can also be a significant influence in the education of your teens.

Students need to see just how big the church truly is, and that requires that all of us youth workers be willing to step outside our comfort zones, preferences, or biases in order to share the responsibility of it.

CORE VALUE: OBSERVATION

As you know, you and I are to live our lives in such a way that teens can make observations from our lives that help them to connect the dots, so to speak. Teens are watching you. They watch the way you interact with others, they watch the way you interact with Scripture, they watch the way you engage the mission of God through acts of justice and through your evangelistic efforts. You and I, as living observations, are to reveal what it means to be Christian, missional, and holy.

CORE VALUE: IMAGINATION

Evoking the imagination or the mind's eye of teens is critical in the process of Christian formation. Teens need to be able to "see" what it looks like for the world to live out the intended ways of God. Teens also need permission and guidance in dreaming how they might more fully live in accordance with God's mission. It is important that we find ways to fire the imagination (through storytelling, art, movies, images, icons, etc.) and allow our students to dream. Do the teens in your group know the importance of engaging their imagination for the sake of their Christian formation, and for the sake of their world?

Youth work includes a lot of fun. However, we are ultimately doing more than providing lock-ins, messy game nights, creative videos, or trips to the local amusement parks. Those activities have their place; there's nothing wrong with doing them. For if it were not for those types of activities, we would struggle to develop meaningful relationships. These special events and activities build stronger bonds with teens and help form lasting, positive memories. However, intentional times of transformation must also happen before we can accomplish our goal of helping open up new dimensions of the soul—transforming squares into cubes and circles into cylinders.

Read and reflect on these important words from a teenager:

A youth ministry leader needs to know that Bible studies and genuine conversations are what get through to teens. It seems that a lot of youth leaders think that teens are only looking to have fun, but that isn't always the case. Yes, pizza parties and games are fun ways to spend time and get to know one another, but this can't be the main focus of the group. A good ministry leader should be able to have fun but know when it is time to sit down and have a godly discussion.

Most importantly, youth ministry leaders must be able to relate to the teens in their group. I have found it helpful when my youth leaders talk about their childhood and teenage years because it is really helpful and motivating to hear about times that they have struggled like I currently am. It is also motivating to hear that although my youth leaders have had some hard times and have not only gotten through them, but have gotten through them and come to God.

I want my leaders to be able to tell me when I am doing something wrong and help me find ways to fix it. Teens are getting very close to adulthood, and we don't always want sugar-coated responses to problems in our lives. Sometimes we need to hear things that we don't always want to hear because they will help us grow into Christians who want to be good role models and live the Christian life.

Youth leaders who are genuine and know how to talk to us are the ones that make the most impact on our lives. As a teen, it is good to know that I can go to someone and that they will care about my problems and help me through them. Although many of my problems may seem small, they are huge obstacles in my life that I need help getting past, and my youth leaders are one of the most important resources that can help me through rough times.

—Will, 16

His divine power has given us everything we need for a godly life through our knowledge of him who called us by his own glory and goodness. Through these he has given us his very great and precious promises, so that through them you may participate in the divine nature, having escaped the corruption in the world caused by evil desires. For this very reason, make every effort to add to your faith goodness; and to goodness, knowledge; and to knowledge, self-control; and to self-control, perseverance; and to perseverance, godliness; and to godliness, mutual affection; and to mutual affection, love. For if you possess these qualities in increasing measure, they will keep you from being ineffective and unproductive in your knowledge of our Lord Jesus Christ. But whoever does not have them is nearsighted and blind, forgetting that they have been cleansed from their past sins.

(2 Peter 1:3-9)

CHAPTER 3

UNDERSTANDING TODAY'S TEENAGER

It goes without saying, but Jesus was once a teenager. I'm sure he was full of the same self-conscious biology and natural emotions that every adolescent deals with. Even though very little is written about Jesus' adolescence, Jesus understands what it means to be a teen. Jesus has first-hand experience.

In addition, God's story is full of young people empowered and equipped by God to do remarkable things:

- Outlandish fashion plate Joseph achieved high office and rescued his people.
- A very young David slew the giant.
- Hot-tempered Moses led the Israelites from captivity into freedom.
- Mary found herself pregnant by the Holy Spirit and gave birth to Jesus, God the Son.

If you think back to your own teenage years, you probably remember times when everything seemed uncomfortable, as well as other moments when everything seemed to click. While the finer points of your teenage years may be different from your students', yours were just as momentous. That kind of reflection enables you to more deeply appreciate the intellectual, physical, emotional, social, and spiritual hurdles this generation faces and gain valuable empathy for the teens you serve. Such understanding and empathy can transcend any generation gap.

Take a moment to read and reflect on the following:

I'll be honest—it was annoying to be a teenager and always have someone over me in some way, shape, or form. It made me feel like I was young, and that's a negative when most high school kids just want to get to the next stage of their lives. I even hated it when people called me *buddy*—it's like a little-kid term that reminded me of my age.

But it also sucks to be an adult right now. The freedom you wanted as a teenager doesn't mean what you thought it would. I remember my youth leader telling me about the dangers of credit cards, and I thought it was a bunch of baloney. Now I look back on those words and respect that instruction, even if it's in hindsight.

I guess that's something I'd tell youth workers—that teenagers can take your words as talking down to them, even when you're not. It's easy for teens to get stuck in the moment and believe that what you went through as a teen has nothing to do with where they are today. Later, though, they'll realize that the wisdom and relationships you offered us were something they took for granted.

I appreciate the community I had as a high school student in a youth ministry because it's not always there for me now. It really was both a time of safety and a home I didn't realize was as special as it was.

—*Brandon, 22*

TEENAGE BRAIN DEVELOPMENT

Did you know that the average brain isn't fully developed until about age 25? That means that some of the things for which we begrudge teenagers are absolutely naturally occurring.[2] For example, if we ask questions and they reply, "Um…I don't know," there's a good chance they really *don't* know. Since mental development and wisdom lags behind teens' physical development, very adult-looking bodies are commonly driven by very shortsighted minds.

On a retreat a few years ago, a teen jumped off the roof of a three-story cabin and broke his arm, leg, and a few ribs. Here's how our post-leap conversation went:

Me: What were you thinking?
Teen: I don't know.
Me: No, seriously, why did you jump off the roof?
Teen: I don't know.
Me: Your mom will ask me why you jumped off the roof. What should I tell her?

---

2. Barbara Strauch, *The Primal Teen: What the New Discoveries about the Teenage Brain Tell Us about Our Kids* (Anchor Books, 2003).

Teen: Tell her I don't know why!

Me: Were you pushed? Were you wrestling with someone?

Teen: No, I just jumped.

Me: Why?

Teen: I don't know.

EMT now on the scene.

EMT: Why did you jump?

Teen: I don't know!

You've probably engaged in similar conversations with teens.

TEENAGE BODY DEVELOPMENT

While some cope well with adolescence and puberty, others find the significant changes to their bodies have a profound effect on them. Teenage males who experience puberty early are more likely to have a positive self-image whereas late developers are more likely to experience pessimistic attitudes. In contrast, females who reach puberty early are more likely to experience depression and anxiety and are generally less satisfied with their weight and appearance compared to late-developing females.

Consider this challenge from Danny Brierley, author of *What Every Volunteer Youth Worker Should Know*:

> As a volunteer youth worker, you need to recognize how young people may react to these changes, both in your one-on-one investments and in the way your youth program will affect them. For example, a competition-based model that includes sports-related activities can heighten comparison with peers with regard to physical appearance and performance. Team games can be less threatening than individual tests, but if young people don't know each other they may struggle working together. Special trips to the beach may be unhelpful for many young people who are embarrassed to be in a bathing suit, and sleeping with peers in the same room can create problems for those who can't control their nighttime snoring or spotting of the bed."

The more you understand what your students are going through, the more you can plan for them to experience positive moments within the context of your ministry to them. And while these memories aren't always transformational in and of themselves, they do tend to create a sense of openness within teens to receive God's Word without defense. As the saying goes, people don't care how much you know until they know how much you care.

ENVIRONMENTS FOR TEENAGE DEVELOPMENT

Like all humans, teens are shaped by the world in which they grow up. And it's our responsibility to understand the cultural context in which we serve students and their families. One of the key factors to understanding today's teenager is to develop the skill of what I and many others refer to as *cultural exegesis*—very simply, the analysis and interpretation of the particular and immediate customs of your society. To exegete culture is to study, explore, and evaluate the very dynamics that make up the culture in which you live and practice your faith. We do this to understand how our culture "works" and discover how God is at work around us. This is key to understanding the teens in your church and community and how to reach and teach them in the most relevant ways.

Some helpful hints for you to begin the process of exegeting the teen culture in your church and community:

- ask a lot of questions (provided on the next page);
- read local middle school/high school newspapers or newsletters;
- visit school Web sites weekly;
- make nonjudgmental observations at public places where students hang out such as the mall or parks, etc.;
- read your teens' blogs/Facebook pages;
- visit local schools (substitute teach, be a consistent spectator at sporting events, attend graduations and ceremonies, band concerts, etc.).

As a youth worker, you are a missionary. Missionaries know the importance of identifying the cultural makeup before they can truly reach indigenous people with the gospel. You, too, should do the hard work of exegeting your cultural context.

For a few years I've been using a questions tool I developed alongside some of my friends and ministry partners to help youth workers exegete their cultures. Take a few moments and work your way through this exegesis process. (NOTE: This is something you should do at least once a month. Also, feel free to develop your own set of questions and share them with other volunteer and paid youth workers. You might even ask your church leaders to do something similar in order to better understand the cultural context in which they serve the community. And don't forget transformational youth ministry seeks to shape the entire person.)

INTELLECTUAL

How are students choosing to learn and discover new information?
How have the ways students learn changed in the last 10 to 15 years?
How does your community value knowledge and education?
What do students in your community do after graduation?

PHYSICAL AND EMOTIONAL

What characterizes your male students' appearance?
What characterizes your female students' appearance?
What shapes your students' self-image the most?
What are the most stressful situations your students face?

SPIRITUAL

What factors influence your students' spiritual development the most?
What spiritual questions are your students asking?
In what areas of spirituality do your students doubt?
In what areas have you seen your students growing spiritually?

SOCIAL

What main issues, needs, or factors in your community are influencing students?
How do social pressures affect students in your community?
What activities (sports or otherwise) are your students most involved in?
In what ways are you seeing a rise in student volunteerism?

It's also important for you to keep up on trends that may or may not impact your particular ministry context. Obviously the Internet is an immense source of data for keeping up with global, national, and regional trends that most likely impact your context in some way. Google terms such as *Teenage Trends* or *Top 10 Trends in Teenage Culture,* etc., and you'll quickly be overwhelmed with data on teenage culture.

PLEASE BE CAREFUL

A few weeks ago I was facilitating a workshop in New Jersey, leading people through the just-outlined exegesis process. During it I observed that nearly every statement about youth in this particular city was rendered in negative terms. It's true that there's much about teenage culture that leaves us wanting, but as advocates we must remain optimistic about teenagers. Every generation has issues, and today's teenagers are no exception—but this isn't the fault of today's teenagers! Please be careful to not project negative assumptions and perceptions on them.

I was on a shuttle bus the other day headed from an airport terminal to a rental car lot. The gentleman sitting next to me saw the book I was reading and said, "So, you work with kids?" I said, "Yes, I work with teens at my church."

"I don't know how you do it," he said. "Today's teens are so wicked! I have a son who is 15 and he is worthless."

My heart sank into my stomach. I have kids, three of them in fact, and I would never call any of them "worthless." And beyond that, even if my kids were worthless, whose fault is that? Am I not the one responsible for raising them? I was sad for this man. He must have an unfortunate relationship with his son. I responded: "I don't think teens are all that bad. And if they were, whose fault would it be? Where do you think they are learning how to live? You and me."

We definitely have challenging days ahead. The world is quickly changing. I'm still optimistic, however, that teenagers can develop a powerful and lasting relationship with God, self, and others. I'm also convinced that youth workers have the ultimate privilege (along with parents) to equip a generation of teens to change the world.

I'm not a sociologist, and I'm not an expert on culture. I am, however, very interested in exegeting culture, especially the culture in which I serve. I believe that our participation in God's mission to restore the world to its intended wholeness requires that youth workers become more culturally aware and sensitive. This doesn't mean we need degrees in sociology (although that might not be a bad idea) to be effective, but it does mean we need to become increasingly aware of the changes in our contexts.

CHAPTER 4

UNDERSTANDING OUR ROLES AND RESPONSIBILITIES

Have you ever considered the stunning absurdity of the first chapter of Acts?

> Then they gathered around him and asked him, "Lord, are you at this time going to restore the kingdom to Israel?"
>
> He said to them: "It is not for you to know the times or dates the Father has set by his own authority. But you will receive power when the Holy Spirit comes on you; and you will be my witnesses in Jerusalem, and in all Judea and Samaria, and to the ends of the earth."
>
> After he said this, he was taken up before their very eyes, and a cloud hid him from their sight.
>
> (Acts 1:6-9)

As the resurrected Jesus stood before his disciples, they were undoubtedly charged up by what they were experiencing. Instead of having his disciples burst forth in the energy of the moment, Jesus had them wait and pray together for the Holy Spirit to come upon them in power.

Being fully God, Jesus knew things about them that they hadn't come to realize yet—from the role they were to play in establishing the kingdom of God to the help of the Holy Spirit they would need to do it.

That isn't the absurd part, however. Since Jesus was fully God, that means he was fully aware of all the disciples' deficiencies and every messed-up way they would attempt to live life and take part in ministry. Not only could Jesus forecast their powerful words that would change nations of people (Acts 2), but also he knew they would fall into limited judgments about each other (Acts 10-11).

So here's the real question: *Why did Jesus entrust his church to disciples (including us) whom he knew were inadequate?*

Ministry is wonderfully messy, made up of a union of the divine with the non-divine...the infinite with the finite...the perfect with the imperfect. As such, youth work has great days and hard days, and some days when we fall short of the ideal—when we wonder if it's worth doing at all.

But there are also days when we get things right and teens engage their faith and enter into a new eternity and way of living—when we help them hear the voice of God, and they soon become adults who walk with Christ. Perhaps you'll even know the delight of standing next to teens in a pool of water as they go public with their faith through baptism, telling witnesses about the transformation Jesus made in their lives. Stay in youth ministry for a while, and you may get emails or text messages from teens about how they've just shared their faith with friends. Nothing is more rewarding than experiencing the contagious power of God transforming lives.

Jesus knows when we're eager to partner with him and yield to the Holy Spirit. Because of this Jesus is willing to entrust us with God's mission—a privilege and responsibility. Yet Jesus also knew how much the disciples would fall short—and he certainly knows how much we do. So if he has faith in you, then maybe you should have faith in you, too.

THE BRUTAL REALITY

I've seen a pattern in youth work that perhaps you've noticed, too. It can be a bit of a blow to your ego if you're not careful; hopefully it's simply a strategic tool you intentionally use to keep you humble. The brutal reality is this...*many of the teens you serve won't necessarily like you or even want to connect with you.*

That might sound harsh, and it doesn't mean that other kids won't love you for who you are. As you stay in youth ministry year after year, you'll develop and maintain amazing relationships with many students. But a large number of young people don't come and participate in what you're offering because of who you are, how cool you think you are, etc. Teens come for other reasons. Consider a few of these motivations for why kids might be in your youth ministry:

- **Parental pressure:** Many kids dread the tension with their parents if they don't take part in church, so they come to whatever their households "require" to put in their time and avoid conflict. In some cases this is productive in the same way that being required to attend school exposes kids to things they need to learn. In other ways, this motivation can become negative if no one breaks through the student's folded arms.

- **Safe place:** It's common for teenagers to seek a safe place to get away from the chaotic people/environments in their lives. While a youth ministry can and should offer this, some students are there to avoid being somewhere else.
- **Faith in other faces:** If you have at least a handful of teenagers whom new students recognize, they may simply put faith in those peers' faces and their choices to attend youth group. This isn't a principle bound by numbers, either, for even just one familiar person can give credibility to an otherwise awkward experience. The young person just starting out may look around and think, *Well, if* they're *here, it must be okay.*
- **Desire to look good:** With the process of getting into a college becoming more competitive, it's not uncommon for young people to cite church involvement on their applications in order to gain an advantage. Of course, some use involvement for present-day favor as well, believing it makes them morally superior to others.
- **Boredom:** Perhaps the most self-explanatory of all these motivations, some kids are simply bored and view whatever you're offering as better than the alternatives. You also may see variations of this where students who want nothing to do with God or religion come to mock your attempts to authentically share about who God is.

Hopefully this better illustrates the challenging truth that not every kid to whom you're attempting to minister likes you or wants a relationship with you. Again, if you're not careful, this can become a negative in your life. If kids don't show up to the things you've prepared and planned, never return your phone calls or emails or text messages, and seem to want nothing to do with you, it can be tempting to take it personally. Of course the other side of the coin is this: If they do come, bring their friends, and seem as though they're your personal groupies, you can begin feeding off that in ways that also incorrectly define your sense of worth.

The thing about followers (whether teenagers or adults) is that they can be erratic and indecisive, demanding much and giving little. If the goal were to get them to follow you, you'd undoubtedly feel that burden. God's plan, though, is for God to lead…and that's something even God's own people have been getting wrong for years.

A LITTLE ABOUT LEADERSHIP

When it came to external appeal, the Israelites found Saul a great choice for their very first human king. The Bible states he was "as handsome a young man as could be found in Israel, and he was a head taller than anyone else" (1 Samuel 9:2). None of the surrounding nations were led by an invisible God; they had human leaders. So God's people reasoned that they could be a better nation if they had a king they could see as opposed to one (God) they couldn't.

Take a step back to the chapter before all of this unfolded, though. In it you see God's preferred ideal—God as ruler of his people with human representatives who prophetically guide them on God's behalf:

> So all the elders of Israel gathered together and came to Samuel at Ramah. They said to him, "You are old, and your sons do not walk in your ways; now appoint a king to lead us, such as all the other nations have."
>
> But when they said, "Give us a king to lead us," this displeased Samuel; so he prayed to the LORD. And the LORD told him: "Listen to all that the people are saying to you; it is not you they have rejected, but they have rejected me as their king. As they have done from the day I brought them up out of Egypt until this day, forsaking me and serving other gods, so they are doing to you. Now listen to them; but warn them solemnly and let them know what the king who will reign over them will claim as his rights."
>
> (1 Samuel 8:4-9)

It's human nature to follow with our eyes rather than our souls, which is why the Israelites ultimately rejected the Lord's warning and God allowed the consequences. Unfortunately, following a leader you can see doesn't mean that leader's motives are as pure as the motives of a God you can't see. It's a tradeoff many make in the moment and later regret when the "ideal" leader is revealed to be less ideal than originally assumed.

Even Saul later realized his role had gone to his head, for by opening himself up to the positive words of the people he simultaneously allowed their negative voices to be louder than they should have been. He once confessed, "I have sinned. I violated the LORD's command and your instructions. I was afraid of the men and so I gave in to them" (1 Samuel 15:24). It's difficult to listen to the voice of God when you've turned your ears toward the crowd. Which begs the question…which are you most tuned into?

WHAT'S THE LOUDEST VOICE IN THE ROOM?

Right now, somebody is expecting you to do something. You feel it, don't you? It may be why you're reading this book or why you can't get rid of the feeling that you aren't living up to whatever potential you sense has been defined for you. The expectant person may be someone supervising you, such as a pastor, elder, or youth ministry director. It might be someone alongside you, such as a fellow volunteer or a parent of a teenager. It could also be a student you shepherd.

In different churches in which I've served, I've felt those expectations from every angle. Some people wanted me to improve student ministry attendance numbers and made it clear that was the goal of my service to the church. On the other extreme, I've had parents take me aside and tell me I should invest into their kids instead of other kids who would be of "little productive use to the kingdom." Likewise I've lost count of the number of young people I've "let down" because I couldn't deliver on the expectations they placed on my time or abilities.

Hear this clearly: There is a youth worker everyone around you wants you to be; but there is a youth worker everyone around you *needs* you to be—and that's the one God has asked you to be. You are full of a burden that God gave you, and God intends to use that burden through teachable moments in the lives of young people… and God doesn't expect you to be someone you're not in order to tell others who he is.

The pressures against you aren't unlike a professional basketball player at the free-throw line with a second left on the clock. But on the other side of that Plexiglas backboard is a crowd of people attempting to distract your attention and concentration—and they need to be blocked out. I've heard that in such moments most basketball players mentally go someplace simple and familiar; they review why they started playing to begin with and the basic mechanics of how they first learned to shoot a ball.

There's something to glean from such wisdom: While blocking out the voices of ministry pressure can seem like an impossible task, it may be as simple as going back to that first instant you felt the burden to do youth work. You may not have known it at the time, but in that moment you were given a picture of "the ball going in"—a sense of what might happen for the greater good of the kingdom if you said "yes" to God's invitation to ministry. So on those days when you're trying to figure out who to listen to, let yourself go back to that place.

SOMEBODY CALLED YOU

Have you ever considered that Jesus called 12 men to be his disciples? Maybe you're aware of the great significance of the number 12 and how it relates to the original tribes of Israel, but it's also simply a number. It signifies that Jesus didn't entrust his ministry into the hands of one person, but into a collective that represented a community of more than 120 (Acts 1:15), which had influence in Jerusalem, Judea, Samaria, and to the uttermost parts of the earth (Acts 1:8).

In other words, God doesn't expect you to do everything yourself. We can never fulfill all the roles we try to fulfill, for there is only so much we can each do. Whether you're the sole volunteer youth worker in the church, oversee a piece of it in some way, or simply invest into a group of kids, God doesn't want you placing pressure on yourself that's meant for God to assume.

You do have a responsibility, though—the healthy burden that compels you to keep doing what God has asked you to do. This is what's commonly referred to as a "calling," and it's one of the biggest areas youth workers struggle with. There are four common ways a calling is first realized:

- **Internal leading:** You felt led by God to enter into ministry. For some this is a moment of clarity or a holy "nudge" within them; others may sense a growing awareness over time from the Holy Spirit as he guides them forward. Even though this is in many ways a personal conversation with God, others who are also solid in the Lord can affirm it.

  > A third time the LORD called, "Samuel!" And Samuel got up and went to Eli and said, "Here I am; you called me." Then Eli realized that the LORD was calling the boy. So Eli told Samuel, "Go and lie down, and if he calls you, say, 'Speak, LORD, for your servant is listening.'" So Samuel went and lay down in his place.

  > The LORD came and stood there, calling as at the other times, "Samuel! Samuel!"

  > Then Samuel said, "Speak, for your servant is listening."

  > (1 Samuel 3:8-10)

- **Communal challenge:** At times, God uses his community to speak a challenge forth so that at least one of its members responds. A church may recognize the need to faithfully invest into the next generation, but without a leader to empower and invest in they may feel directionless. This can be communicated through a general announcement anyone can respond to, or it might resemble the early church in the way its elders appointed people to service who were "full of the Spirit and wisdom" so that ministry could be delegated appropriately.

> In those days when the number of disciples was increasing, the Hellenistic Jews among them complained against the Hebraic Jews because their widows were being overlooked in the daily distribution of food. So the Twelve gathered all the disciples together and said, "It would not be right for us to neglect the ministry of the word of God in order to wait on tables. Brothers, choose seven men from among you who are known to be full of the Spirit and wisdom. We will turn this responsibility over to them and will give our attention to prayer and the ministry of the word."

> (Acts 6:1-4)

- **Supernatural circumstance:** Moses and the burning bush. Balaam and a talking donkey. Mary and Joseph and their conversations with angels. Because something tangible happened to these people, we can find ourselves craving similar supernatural experiences. Nonetheless, as much as God did reveal the calling through supernatural events, he seldom duplicates them. We should never seek the miracle but instead pursue the Miracle Maker.

> When the LORD saw that he had gone over to look, God called to him from within the bush, "Moses! Moses!"

> And Moses said, "Here I am."

> "Do not come any closer," God said. "Take off your sandals, for the place where you are standing is holy ground."

> (Exodus 3:4-5)

- **Emotional burden:** There are those in youth ministry who simply do what they do because they love God and teenagers. While they may not have had a specific direction from the Holy Spirit into this ministry, they understand the general calling from God to be sure that one generation spiritually invests into the next. So while their sense of calling may feel like it lacks some of the bells and whistles of something more supernatural, nothing could be further from the truth. God takes great delight in people who "get it" and become emotionally burdened for kids and the unique challenges they face in becoming Christ-followers.

> I will come and proclaim your mighty acts, Sovereign LORD; I will proclaim your righteous deeds, yours alone. Since my youth, God, you have taught me, and to this day I declare your marvelous deeds. Even when I am old and gray, do not forsake me,

my God, till I declare your power to the next generation, your mighty acts to all who are to come.

(Psalm 71:16-18)

The Bible teaches that all Christians are called into ministry on some level—that we are a priesthood of believers. (1 Peter 2:9) Unless you're a raving egomaniac, you'll probably experience some doubts about your capacity to follow through on such a God-sized task. That's why it's helpful to remember the way God called you to work with students. The more you stay in tune with why you got into this in the first place, the more you'll have a powerful reference point on days when ministry is especially hard.

And it will be. Some days you will wonder how you can manage it all when there's so much in your own life that seems out of control. Again, if you were meant to be the person students are to follow, you'd eventually run out of energy and burn up. Out of all the hats you will wear, though, God will never ask you to wear his.

THE VARIOUS ROLES WE PLAY

Let's talk about that for a minute. Just how many hats do you wear? Somewhere along the margin of this page, write down as many of the hats as you can think of that you wear as a volunteer youth worker. If there's another person nearby (e.g., a friend, your spouse, or a fellow youth worker), do this exercise with that person. Take a moment to complete it now.

Let me guess—you came up with roles such as *teacher, coach, cheerleader, chef, chauffeur, janitor, mentor, banker, referee, parent, mediator, punching bag, friend, counselor, event planner, tutor,* and so on and so on. If you spent enough time you probably could fill every page in this book.

Youth workers are shepherds. We shepherd students through shared experiences and help them mature into missional people. To shepherd, in its simplest definition, is to tend, guide, care for, and protect. This is what we do for our students. This isn't news to you, I'm sure. But what does it really mean to be a shepherd? Sometimes it's difficult to know what it looks like on a practical level to tend, guide, care for, and protect our students.

Here's a great description of a shepherd:

In early morning he led forth the flock from the fold, marching at its head to the spot where they were to be pastured. Here he watched them all day, taking care that none of the sheep strayed, and if any for a time eluded his watch and wandered away from the rest, seeking diligently till he found and brought it back. In those lands sheep require to be supplied regularly with water, and the shepherd for this purpose has to guide them either to some running stream or to wells dug in the wilderness and furnished with troughs. At night, he brought the flock home to the fold, counting them as they passed under the rod at the door to assure himself that none were missing. Nor did his labors always end with sunset. Often he had to guard the fold through the dark hours from the attack of wild beasts, or the wily attempts of the prowling thief (see 1 Samuel 17:34).[3]

Keeping that description in mind, what does it mean to shepherd as a youth worker? In other words, what are the specific roles you play? (We do a ton, eh? At times it's overwhelming.)

One way to understand our role as shepherd is to view what we do as part of being advocates, advisors, and guides. These three roles have everything to do with infusing our students with God's narrative and mission and developing them into story-formed students. I contend that youth workers shepherd their students best when leaders see themselves as embodying all three of these roles, not just one or two.

ADVOCATE

An *advocate* can be defined as one who stands in the gap, cheers on, and speaks in support of another. The advocate is not unlike a coach—an encourager, an opportunity provider, one who helps students grow and develop and go deeper in their faith. *But true advocating can occur only when there is depth to the relationship.* And the greatest thing youth ministry has going for it is its potential to support healthy relationships—and yet the most difficult thing about youth ministry is cultivating healthy relationships! You can be a good advocate only when you have established healthy relationships with students.

Healthy relationships consist of several key aspects: love, selflessness, care, listening, and so on. But regardless of how you might define a healthy relationship, without spending time and sharing proximity with a person, you can't even begin to assume a humble presence in someone's life. Transformational youth ministry is about genuine relationships with students.

ADVISOR

An *advisor* can be defined as one who gives advice and guidance—not unlike a counselor or mentor for a student. Someone who's there to give advice and assist in

---

3. http://www.christiananswers.net/dictionary/shepherd.html

the decision-making process; not an "answer giver" but a partner with the student in the practice of counseling. *But true counseling can occur only when there's discernment stemming from the depth of shared experiences.* What will make you a great shepherd is how well you discern how to help students determine the next right thing to do in their lives. And you can only be an effective co-discerner when you:

- are in tune with God's narrative and mission;
- have a deep relationship with students; and
- discover how to discern appropriately based on the experiences of your own life and story.

GUIDE

A *guide* can be defined as one who shows the way by directing, leading, and serving as a model. Not unlike an adventure guide for students—someone who's walking the journey with them, pointing out things along the way, and allowing them to enjoy and encounter the learning that naturally comes from the journey (and giving directions when needed). *But true guiding can happen only in the context of ongoing shared experiences built upon deep relationships and moments of helpful discernment.*

THE UNPREDICTABILITY OF YOUTH MINISTRY

Youth work will regularly surprise and call things out of you that you don't expect. It doesn't matter how many years you've been doing it, for each day holds some unplanned variable within it. There will be times when some of your most spiritually solid kids make destructive choices and need perspective, just as there will be days when kids with questions need help standing firm on answers. You just never know what the day will bring.

Of all the roles you play in a student's life, your greatest ability is your *availability*. At times you'll be like a cop, policing hard situations with strong instruction; or like a cheerleader, encouraging the potential in young people that they cannot see; or like a daytime talk show counselor, listening to relationship problems on the fly and offering guidance to help foster reconciliation; or a host of other roles that include things you do *with* teens as well as things you do *for* them.

Not every student will understand what you're trying to do, but keep doing what you're doing. It's often the little moments of consistency that you forget about that they remember later. I can't tell you how many phone calls, emails, and conversations I've had over the years in which students from years ago affirmed the difference God made in their lives through me—and almost always in a way that was more spontaneous and personal than it was planned and structured. A formal lesson may have truth in it, but your godly life lived out in front of students is an investment unlike any other.

And let your attitude be contagious, sharing some of these stories with others in your life who may catch the vision. There's no better recruiter for youth work than another volunteer taking part in God's dream and loving it. If there's a paid staff member in your church (i.e., the lead pastor or youth pastor), everyone expects that individual to recruit volunteers. When you put it out there, though, others around you will feel a unique motivation to consider it.

Speaking of which, if no one has yet told you the following, allow me the honor:

- <u>You</u> are the right person to love the students in your midst into a deeper connection with God.
- <u>You</u> are the real deal—imperfections and all—and will challenge other adults to invest, mentor, coach, disciple, and shepherd in a way that's natural to their unique bents.
- <u>You</u> have more credibility in Jesus than you realize to strike up conversations with teenagers who seem to have endless supplies of brick and mortar for constructing relational walls, and…
- <u>You</u> will say the right thing at just the right time to break through because God will speak through you as you allow him to.
- <u>You</u> are not alone.

So many people are in your corner, including God. He won't leave you to fight the good fight alone, so be sure to invest in your relationship with him. Remember…it seems easier to do ministry for others on adrenaline than to do the hard, sweaty work of spending time growing yourself. You're not a commodity God wants to use and dispose of, though—so do things his way, and you'll end up feeling the right way.

PART TWO

FOUNDATIONS OF YOUTH MINISTRY II: RELATIONSHIPS AND PARTNERSHIPS

CHAPTER 5

WORKING WITH INDIVIDUALS

My favorite movie is *Good Will Hunting*. Will Hunting (Matt Damon) is a janitor at MIT and possesses an astonishing (and at first, unapplied) intelligence and aptitude, particularly for mathematics. Beneath his blue-collar exterior and heritage is a genius with a photographic memory that many, including his closest friends, wish he would use professionally so he could leave his humble situation and make a better life for himself.

Will gets in a bit of trouble with the law, and in exchange for his release, he's directed by the court to receive counseling for his anger and violent tendencies. His therapist is Sean Maguire (Robin Williams), an instructor at a local community college.

Will and Sean have some things in common, as they're both from blue-collar backgrounds and are equally stubborn in regard to moving on with their lives (Sean lost his wife to cancer). Through the development of a unique friendship, both Will and Sean are forced to deal with their pasts and futures.

There are many wonderful scenes in the movie, but none is more profound to me than when Sean finally breaks through to Will, helping him realize that his past is not his fault. Will has made some errors in judgment along the way, but the issues that haunt Will have nothing to do with who Will is but rather with the adults who've surrounded him. In the end, Will chooses to chase his dream, leaving all he knows behind in order to find a new future. His closest friends are surprised by his decision but thrilled about his opportunity to experience a new life.

Good Will Hunting is filled with redemptive moments. It's packed with powerful scenes that inspire me every time I watch it. And Sean, the therapist—patient, truthful, and forgiving—greatly inspires me. He's able to listen and humbly learn from his patient Will, also choosing to embark on a renewed life.

Call me crazy, but the movie reminds me of my role as a shepherd for teens. It reminds me of the characteristics required to cultivate and sustain meaningful relationships with them. It also reminds me of my own stubbornness and selfishness, reminding me to move past myself in order to focus on others' needs.

Youth ministry is a lot like *Good Will Hunting*. It's full of redemption, mentoring, love, therapy, intimacy, humor, fear, hope, pain, celebration, friendship, compassion, and triumph—and then some. Which is why it's imperative that we develop meaningful relationships with teens and other adult leaders.

KEY TRAITS FOR CONNECTING WITH TEENS

My friend Mark is a pastor of a church in Colorado. We worked on the same staff at a church in Minneapolis for a year or so. Mark has the uncanny ability to connect with everyone he comes in contact with. I've never seen one time when Mark failed to begin or maintain a friendship. He walks in the room, and people just start liking him—it's disgusting! Some of us have to work super hard to break out of our introversion just to have conversations; but Mark meets someone at a gas station, and they're lifelong friends.

Obviously that's a bit of an embellishment. Mark does, however, possess certain traits that make him wonderful at building relationships—especially with those with whom he's built longer connections.

I studied Mark (and others like him) to learn what makes him so good at connecting with teens. I discovered that people like Mark understand at least 14 things that allow them to build meaningful relationships. I believe each of us should practice and develop these 14 traits when establishing relationships with teens in our churches and communities:

1. **The importance of being yourself.** You only need to be you! Teens don't want you to pretend to be who you aren't. They sniff straight through inauthenticity and quickly dismiss adults who try to look cool or act hip. Teens want genuine relationships with genuine people.

2. **The significance of accepting people for who they are.** If there's one thing teens hate, it's being judged. Many adults I know are quick to judge students

according to the clothes they wear, the music on their mp3 players, the books they read, the cars they drive, where they work, who they hang out with, etc. If you want to connect with teens, evaluate them only after you get to know them. (Of course to tell you not to judge is just silly. We all judge, despite what the Bible commands—Luke 6:37. But can you at least wait to evaluate them until you really know them?)

3. **The need to go beyond just doing well to loving well.** Doing good things for people is just that—good. Teens want to be loved deeply. They want to be cared for and appreciated, just like any other human being (or animal for that matter). Not long ago a student in my small group was given a new shirt, with price tag and all. After the adult who had given the shirt to the teen left, the teen threw the shirt in the garbage. I asked her why she threw it away, and she said, "I don't want a shirt from her. She's only giving me a shirt because she doesn't like the ones I wear." This teen didn't want a shirt; she wanted to be loved for who she was. I don't know the motives of that giver in this case, but I know the perceptions of the receiver.

4. **The relevance of asking questions.** Most teens I know won't say a whole lot to adults unless they're asked questions. But after being asked questions, they usually respond respectfully. Asking interesting questions can help eliminate some of the awkward moments at the beginning of conversations. (Note: Don't ask yes-or-no questions unless you're okay getting yes-or-no answers— and I would be prepared with more than one question if you expect to hold a conversation with a teen.)

5. **The importance of remembering people's names and things about them.** We've all either been the person who says, "I remember your face, but I can't place your name"—or know someone who's been that person. Well, with teens, that doesn't cut it. *They want to know that you know their names.* Not only that, but they want to know what you remember about them. Names are easily memorized; interests change, however. So merely memorize an interest of one of your teens, and you'll risk that teen not having that interest the next time you meet him or her. So be in conversation with them frequently enough to know how their interests are changing. That's when they'll be appreciative.

6. **The importance of transparency.** Be honest with teens. They know when you aren't being honest or transparent with them. Don't hide anything from them and make it a priority to live your life as an open book.

7. **The meaning of a real compliment.** Teens can sniff out a fake compliment sooner than anyone. If you intend to say, "I like your shirt," or "You played great tonight," or "I like your new tattoo," or whatever, be sure you mean it. Teens hear genuine compliments so infrequently that when you do give them honest, meaningful compliments, they'll go a long way. They'll remember them, that's for sure.

8. **The importance of laughing at yourself.** Don't take yourself too seriously. Be okay with embarrassment and awkward situations that you might find yourself in. Laughing at yourself can create a carefree and positive atmosphere that fuels teens' sense of freedom and authentic amusement.

9. **The value of flexibility.** I learned really early on in youth ministry that nothing ever goes as expected. Being flexible and adaptable are keys to maintaining your sanity (assuming it's still intact) and the overall health of your youth ministry environment. Inflexible youth workers usually don't last long as youth workers.

10. **The importance of a humble posture.** I've seen youth workers who have a hard time relating to teens simply because of how they "view" themselves in comparison to teens. The "when I was your age" statements and the "just wait, you'll learn the hard way" proclamations detract from your ability to truly relate to teens. Now, you don't have to (and shouldn't) act like a teen or artificially lower your age and maturity level, but you will need to take a humble and caring posture to truly relate.

11. **The significance of reliability.** As much as it's within your control, be sure to keep your commitments and do what you say you're going to do. If you tell a teen you'll visit him at work, you'd better head over there and get yourself a taco. If you tell a teen you'll be at one of her games before the season ends, you'd better find a way to get there. Not only do teens need to see reliability modeled, they need to feel it modeled.

12. **The opportunity of reaching out to others.** People with the ability to build meaningful relationships look for ways to reach out and help where needed or where they can be present.

13. **The true desire to listen carefully.** How well do you listen? Are you able to truly listen to others when they speak to you? In order to build meaningful relationships, you must discipline yourself to listen well if you don't already.

14. **The importance of participating in others' lives**. It's one thing to be available at a regularly scheduled event or preplanned program, but making your-

self available to others and participating in their lives outside of "normal" times are crucial to building authentic relationships. It can be very hard to participate in the lives of teens, but finding meaningful ways to do so is hugely significant to the health of your overall ministry.

A RELATIONAL PROCESS FOR SPIRITUAL DEEPENING

Your purpose in listening and connecting with teens through relationships is to love them without an agenda. Part of loving teens is offering them opportunities to go deeper with God by understanding more about God, themselves, and others.

Your relationship with the teens in your ministry will model a process of spiritual discovery and growth. It will help them progress from feeling like awkward strangers with you (and God) to gaining a sense that they are understood by you (and God).

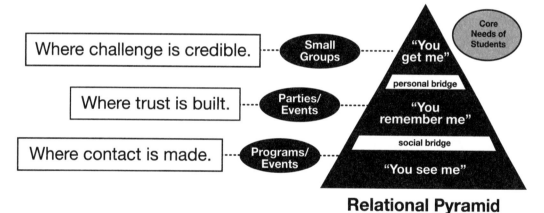

Relational Pyramid

Each level of the Relational Pyramid represents a different stage of relational progression that can foster lasting transformation:

LEVEL 1: "YOU SEE ME."

Your goal at this level is to make contact with a wide range of people. This can be done through programs or events that help students feel "seen" through how you speak to them and with them. Everything plays into this, from the people you put on a stage on a youth night to the intentional ways teenagers feel reached out to by their peers and adult leaders.

Social bridge: There should be an easy on-ramp of sorts to help students feel empowered to take the next step in. Maybe it's at a youth night where a new student is invited into an inner circle of relationships so that he or she isn't left alone in the back row. The more social bridges you help form, the more you help make it possible to learn facts about the student that transition into the next step.

LEVEL 2: "YOU REMEMBER ME."

An initial level of trust is built when you give young people reasons to believe you're paying attention to their lives. It can start small as you ask them about specific things in their lives that are important to them (e.g., athletics, academics, movies, jobs, etc.) and then progress further as they open up about more critical things (e.g., tests at school they're worried about, something happening in their homes, etc.). You can nurture this on a larger scale by facilitating fun parties or grouping students into teams (which is especially helpful if you serve in a larger ministry). Regardless of the environment, make certain to be intentional about using their names and asking them about things they shared with you in previous conversations.

Personal bridge: Now that you know something about your students, you can start to invite them into opportunities with God that are specific to their interests. For instance, if you've made contact with a teen who's a budding musician, there may be a place for him/her to play on your church praise team. Or if you know some students who enjoy amusement parks, ask them to help you plan your next group trip. The more ways you can tailor your invitations to kids' unique interests, the more they may be inclined to take a personal step with you (and ultimately with God).

LEVEL 3: "YOU GET ME."

A potentially productive and destructive level; it's up to you to determine which way this will go. Once a young person feels understood by you (and perhaps the small group of peers she's a part of), it will be tempting for her to become dependent upon you instead of God. So let her make use of the pastoral support you offer, but always point her toward Jesus so that true transformation can take place. In other words, use your existing relationship to ensure that any challenge you make is credible as you lead her into a deeper connection with Jesus Christ.

This process will vary with each student to whom we minister—because often students will put up walls of disinterest at our attempts to build relationships with them. But whether or not it's legitimate on their end—or if they're simply testing us—*fully commit ourselves to see our way through the awkward conversations.* It's better to have several conversations that go nowhere than to never try because it seems "too hard" to find a way into their lives.

As you move toward the top of this model, you'll find that the focus shifts from the quantity of connections to the quality of change. Meaning, you may have more connections at the earlier stages of this process but find more significant conversations with the few at the top. It's ideal to have several relationships taking place on all of these levels to ensure both outreach and discipleship are occurring.

Let me repeat: *This is hard stuff.* Don't pretend it won't be. Make several attempts, never give up. Eventually you'll find things to talk to them about and follow up with. If you need an example, you need only look to the constant invitational nature of God. How many times has God tried to build relationships with us, only to have us brush him off? God knows how you feel, the nature of your fears, and what will happen next.

CHAPTER 6

WORKING WITH SMALL GROUPS

Over the years of being involved with youth ministry, I've learned through personal and practical experience that small groups not only are essential for effective youth ministry—and, more specifically, essential for the direct impact of teens' faith formation—small groups are *the most critical*.

Like adults, teens need circles of friends who'll help them experience enduring spiritual discovery and growth. Without circles of friends, community is impossible, and Christian formation is implausible.

Small groups provide the connectivity needed to experience meaningful discovery and growth. Small groups also provide the impetus for friendships, encouragement, problem resolution, accountability, collective prayer, peer ministry, biblical conversation and interpretation, spiritual-gift contributions, authentic community, leadership development, family-oriented worship—the list goes on and on and on.

If you contend, as I do, that the most effective Christian formation is found through the mission of God for the sake of the world, then you have to develop and maintain a commitment to others-centeredness. The mission of God is worked out through the cooperation of a people with their King, not through isolated activities. An essential aspect of answering the question, "What did I sign up for?" has to entail the facilitation of small groups.

Some youth ministries *are* small groups. The number of teens in your faith community may simply mean that you're a small group—meaning that you don't need to break down your youth ministry into smaller communities from a larger body.

For example, a few months ago I was leading a workshop in Lincoln, Nebraska, and a youth worker asked me to help her better strategize for effective small group ministry. I asked her, "How many teens are in your group?" "A little over 200," she responded. Another youth worker asked, "Can you have a small group ministry to seven teens? Cause that's all we have in our church!"

Regardless of the number of teens in your church—500, 50, or 5—the common challenges and characteristics of effective small groups remain the same—as does the biblical basis for utilizing small group ministry in the first place.

COMMON CHALLENGES OF SMALL(ER) GROUP MINISTRY

My experience tells me that nearly every youth ministry deals with very similar challenges in the intentional and strategic emphasis of small groups. While individual ministries might have contextual differences, there still remains a certain set of challenges that threads through all of our ministries. These challenges are certainly the kind that can be overcome, and we'll discuss how we might overcome them—nevertheless, they are challenges that shape the practice of forming effective small groups. Some of these common challenges are:

- Teens who won't say a word.
- Teens who can't sit still.
- Teens who dominate the conversation.
- Teens who attend because they're forced to go—and they hate it.
- There aren't enough volunteers to lead an effective small group ministry.
- It's very hard to find relevant material that fits your particular group of teens.
- You (and other volunteers) have no time to prepare.

Sometimes these and many other challenges can be overwhelming. Often they can be enough for you to want stop strategically thinking about small groups and reverting to what seems easiest—keeping all the teens in one room where you can more effectively manage what often feels like chaos. It's very important, however, to fight the urge to give up small groups as a tactical aspect of your ministry to teens. It's critical that you and I keep in mind the following three potential solutions to our challenges:

1. The biblical basis for small group ministry.
2. The various ways that teens in your group process information.

3. The way you or any other youth workers deliver the content.

THE BIBLICAL BASIS FOR SMALL GROUP MINISTRY

Beginning with the Trinity—specifically the configuration of it—we know that relationships and the working out of relationships among a small group are core values of God. Jesus revealed to us the importance of nurturing a small group of people—his disciples. When it comes time for Jesus to fulfill his work on the cross, he prays for "oneness" among his disciples and the entire church. One of the best ways to develop oneness is through small groups. Throughout the Gospels we see Jesus taking time to strategically create oneness with his disciples—i.e., the "gold standard" of small groups. Also, throughout the New Testament we are challenged with "one another" commands, which bolster the argument for the importance of small groups (where oneness and one-another commands are most conceivably completed).

The early church (Acts 2:42-47) also showed us how small, authentic communities operate, and throughout history people like the Wesley brothers have also shown us the magnitude of small groups—or what they called "holiness clubs." There is, therefore, a biblical/historical basis for small groups that ought to spur us on to build effective small group ministries.

THE VARIOUS WAYS THAT TEENS IN YOUR GROUP PROCESS INFORMATION

It's possible that each teen in your group processes information uniquely—in fact, differently than any other teen in your group. Part of overcoming the obstacles and challenges of small group ministry (especially the challenges of flagging attention spans, learning capacities, dominant or dormant participation, etc.) is understanding that your teens process differently your content as mechanisms for learning (e.g., Bible lessons and studies, videos, movies, music, whatever). People process information in many different ways. Here's a short sampling:

Wondering—to speculate or be curious
("I wonder what it will be like to be in heaven…")
Grasping—to take hold of firmly and wrestle with
("So if what the pastor said is right, then I need to…")
Adapting—to change a former thought
("God, you're so much bigger than I thought…")

Shaping—to mold one thought into a deeper thought
("Now, if this is true, then…")
Theorizing—to conclude based on speculation
("The second someone stands up tonight during music, we'll see everyone else join them, even if they don't want to…")
Calculating—to make alert assessments before concluding
("If I'm going to apply all of this, then I might need to first…")
Condensing—to bond various thoughts
("The main thing I'm taking away from this whole day is…")
Abstracting—to extract or separate various thoughts
("I heard Bob tell me one thing, but Sue told me another…")
Inventing—to develop a brand-new thought
("It's time for us to step out in a new direction, and I think I know what it is…")
Uncovering—to discover a new thought through an old one
("Wow! I never caught something like this before!")
Generalizing—to conclude based on a broad array of thoughts
("From what I know of Scott, I'm guessing we'll start our meeting late tonight…")

Regardless of which process a student engages in, it's our responsibility—along with the other influencers in their lives—to help them become the best learners they are capable of becoming. In fact, I'd argue that the questions young people ask about faith are often more revealing than their conclusions. So instead of asking, *How can I help my students agree with what I'm teaching them?* you need to instead ponder, *How can I help my students critically think their way toward conviction?*

This line of thinking, along with our teens' various processing techniques, means that we're also to concern ourselves with the way you or any other youth workers deliver the content.

THE WAY YOU OR ANY OTHER YOUTH WORKERS DELIVER THE CONTENT

In 2006, I published a book titled *A New Kind of Youth Ministry*. Among many other things it looks at the ways we help our students learn. My intention with *A New Kind of Youth Ministry*, particularly the chapter on learning, is to help push youth workers to think about the differences between the learner-centered environment and teacher-centered learning environment—the former, of course, is governed by what's best for the learners while the latter is governed by what's best for the teacher.

The following is an illustration that helps us notice the difference between these two types of learning environments:

Teacher-centered	Learner-centered
Preferences/Skills of teacher	Needs of student
Static in nature	Always evolving
Breadth	Depth
Rote	Experiential
Solo	Cohort/Peer-to-peer
Product	Process

PREFERENCES/SKILLS OF TEACHER VS. NEEDS OF STUDENT

Youth workers can often fall into the routine of preparing for and executing environments of learning that primarily set them up to perform well. Granted it's crucial that any teacher or youth worker teach effectively. However, the most important aspect of teaching is that learners grasp the content and eventually apply it—the same applies to youth workers who teach.

STATIC IN NATURE VS. ALWAYS EVOLVING

It's widely known that a static learning environment (e.g., Sunday school class, youth group event, worship experience, etc.) leads to learner disinterest and indifference. However, always-evolving environments that are constantly on the move or unpredictable have a greater chance of connecting with students representing a variety of learning types and abilities. (NOTE: This is when knowing your group well is key! The better you know your students, the better you'll help create an effective learning environment. For example, your particular group of teens may share very similar learning styles that might do better with a rote and predictable environment where they gain a sense of understanding through the comfort of knowing that there will be no surprises.)

BREADTH VS. DEPTH

Often youth workers believe they should expose their teens to as much information or knowledge as they can possibly teach. However, there's a good chance that your teens are better suited to learn the things of God by going deep as opposed to wide.

(Again, your exegesis of the group is key.) Ask yourself, *What do my teens need most?* I have spoken to frustrated volunteer youth workers who never get through a full Sunday school lesson. The reality is that you might not need to finish a lesson. Rather, you may need to go deep on just one issue within the lesson instead of trying to be sure all of the teens get all of the content before they leave for the day.

ROTE VS. EXPERIENTIAL

Experiential learning isn't synonymous with interactive learning. Interactive learning may be collaborative and involve others, or it may mean that something is "kinesthetic" (e.g., sketching an image or shaping a figurine with clay). *Experiential* means that the lesson or knowledge being dispersed is actually lived—that it's applied. In addition, rote (or repetitious) learning isn't synonymous with experiential learning, either. Rote memorization, for example, can be helpful, but would you prefer an end goal of a teen quoting a Bible passage or living out the content of that verse? I understand that Bible memory is important, but when it ends with mere recitation of words and isn't applied, such an exercise isn't enough.

SOLO VS. COHORT/PEER-TO-PEER

When we leave teens to learn about God on their own, we set them up for failure. But helping teens learn together, in community, makes for a longer-lasting situation with the greatest opportunity for impact. The benefits of learning in community— such as teens learning about God from each other and being formed in their faith with their peers in the context of relationships—prepare and equip teens for ministry in the church later in life.

PRODUCT VS. PROCESS

I'm so glad that we make disciples and not widgets! How boring would it be if all our students were the same? Youth workers must look beyond "finished products" and instead help those still being formed that the process—the journey itself—is important. Promote patience in your group. Not every teen will engage the faith with the same passion as others. That's okay. As long as teens are in process, I believe God is forming them. (We will talk much further about developing spirituality in a later chapter.)

COMMON CHARACTERISTICS

Beyond common challenges, I've also witnessed over the years that youth ministries that are intentional about developing small groups and stewarding them effectively share common characteristics and outcomes:

- Common ground—a reason to come together
- Clear picture—the purpose of the group
- Community—with a cause; what is your purpose?
- Consistency—meeting time and modeling adults as spiritual influencers
- Connection points—complements other aspects of the ministry
- Care/Compassion—loves others inside and outside the group
- Convergence—diversity of all kinds
- Commitment—led by and yielded to the mission and work of God through the Holy Spirit
- Collective progress and growth—numerical growth as well as spiritual growth
- Celebration—finding meaningful ways to worship God
- Creativity—interactive and experiential learning options
- Communication—authentic, accurate, and truthful

Youth ministries are best sustained in a healthy environment comprised of youth workers who understand the importance of small groups in their ministry.

CHAPTER 7

WORKING WITH PARENTS AND OTHER ADULTS

One unfortunate reality in youth ministry is the frequent disconnect between the youth worker and the other adults in a teen's life. While each party may be aware of the others from afar, often not much effort goes into building bridges to create a set of connections.

Even simple words of appreciation aren't often shared with one another, mainly due to the time constraints and fatigue each individual experiences from investing into teens on their own. This solo approach may earn points for motives, but it's a loser when one considers the overall effectiveness it could have achieved if a network approach was used instead.

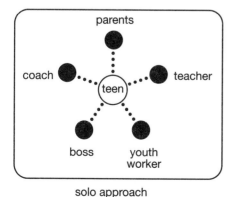

solo approach

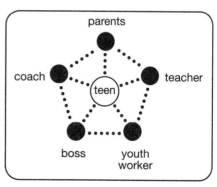

network approach

Another temptation volunteer youth workers face is general indifference toward parents/guardians. Some volunteers even maintain a sense of frustration toward them—why? It flows from volunteers' connections with students, believe it or not. As teens vent about life at home, they typically want you to nod in agreement. Over time this can reactively create judgmental attitudes in youth workers toward parents that can, if left unchecked, work against all the good you're trying to bring about in teens' lives.

Consider how this may or may not be true of you. Have you ever observed a parent's discipline style and concluded you could do a much better job? As you spend time with teenagers, do you believe you know more about them than their "oblivious" parents do? Do you see the broken situation at home and believe your job is to become a substitute father or mother?

Rather, it's your responsibility to see past all the temptations that would push you into this kind of thinking. There will be times when students tell you how you "get them" in ways their parents don't—and that can go to your head if you let it. Just because they're sharing things with you that they aren't sharing with their parents doesn't mean that's the way it's supposed to be. Your role isn't to replace their moms or dads—never; instead it's to partner with their moms and dads. Your role is to help that household fulfill its mission of raising Christ-followers of all ages. If they're struggling with that goal, it isn't time to point your finger but to lend a hand. While many churches complain that parents aren't living up to the mandate to be the spiritual leaders for their kids, they fail to recognize their responsibility to take part in restoring them spiritually to do so.

SORTING THROUGH THE DISORDER

This matter of parenting and familial influence isn't the only area where students move away from adults in their lives. Many young people struggle with dysfunctional relationships with employers, coaches, music instructors, teachers, etc. Each of these relationships flows from structures intended to be blessings to youth but somewhere along the way became about something else.

A family I know has kids who take part in a local school sport and do quite well at it. In fact, the oldest child is so skilled that his coach can't keep up with his abilities. As a result a lot of tension has developed between the coach and the boy's family—not because the family has intentionally stirred things up, but because the family sees the boy's abilities regressing instead of progressing. Further, the teenager often gets snubbed by the coach in ways that most wouldn't notice—but he does just the same, and it continues to set a poor standard for the role an adult could and should play in this boy's life.

Again, in situations like this, it's easy to take the teenager's side and lose perspective on other things going on. But when a student loses trust in one adult, it may be harder for that teen to trust another. If we're not careful, we can begin to see ourselves as commentators on those problems rather than question-askers regarding why the problems exist in the first place. It's one thing to extend compassion and fill in the gap; it's quite another to work on correcting the matter altogether.

You've been empowered and challenged to have a deeper perspective than the average person, and you need to share what you're learning with others. I found that hosting a "parent night" several times each year was helpful toward accomplishing this. The night consisted of a unique program where kids brought their moms and dads so we could share, pray, laugh, and reflect through Scripture on what it means to raise the next generation of Christ-followers.

While we committed ourselves to help parents fulfill their roles as spiritual leaders to their kids, I began realizing that many parents were more interested in the church doing that work for them. Initially this was frustrating on several levels. Then one night I ended up talking with a parent about it and tried to help her understand God's challenge in this way. She became quiet, took a breath, and then quietly confessed: "I want to do that, but I don't know how. My own life is so messed up, and I know very little about the Bible."

There have been other responses to that challenge, though. In the years that I hosted parent nights before I had kids of my own, I would often hear the statement, "That sounds nice, but when you have your own kids, you'll understand." I have to admit I've learned some things about teens by becoming a dad that I otherwise didn't realize. However, none of that has changed—nor will it ever change—what God has commanded and qualified us to do. Don't ever feel like you have to stand on your own experience when the Word of God is a much firmer foundation.

The more the institution of the family has broken down over the years, the more these issues will continue to pop up. You'll encounter divorcing couples who won't talk to each other yet share great interest in their kid—and you'll have to work with both of them. You'll encounter households in which the couple lives together, and yet the boyfriend/girlfriend takes more of a parental role than the student's actual parent; same-sex relationships will begin to become more common, and you may have a homosexual parenting couple who wants to work with you to spiritually invest in a kid they care about. I won't lie to you—working with parents is often more uncomfortable than it is easy.

INITIATE CONTAGIOUS LEARNING

There are many action steps we can take to better partner with parents and other adults. Consider which of these apply to your context:

PLAN IN COMMUNITY

While it may be easier to come up with ideas for your ministry on your own, it's more dynamic to plan events in community. So invite different people to offer ideas, whether you get them all together in one place or connect with them individually. Ask parents, coaches, teachers, and church members what "one thing" they believe would be a blessing to the spiritual lives of students. And after they share their ideas, ask them to pitch in on whatever level they're able and interested.

INCREASE COMMUNICATION

A productive step you can take right now is to write down anything ordinary (and out of the ordinary) happening in the youth ministry over the next three months. Once you do this, photocopy the paper and pass it out; add it into your church's Web site; give the info to the person who makes your church calendar; and so on. Even if everyone knows what's happening, writing it down increases the potential of people planning their schedules around it and asking appropriate questions in a timely manner.

BUILD A RELATIONSHIP

Aside from the interconnectivity you're establishing around working with students, consider investing in friendships with other adults—and just for who they are. Often when it comes to youth workers and contact with other adults, we consider primarily what they can offer us or our ministries—but casual chats and letters of encouragement go a long way toward building foundations for life-change in those people, too. Even planning an extra 10 minutes before and after your gatherings to connect with parents can go a long way.

PROVIDE PERSPECTIVE

As you find different resources that spiritually bless you and your understanding of young people, share them with parents and your growing network of adults. Send out emails that announce media they should pay attention to; find out what great books your library carries and make a list of suggested reading material; create or download Internet audio that parents can access and grow from. Whether this is all new to you, or you consider yourself well resourced, share the journey.

CREATE MENTORING CONNECTIONS

Within your church and other churches are people who've successfully navigated the parenting journey. Bring them together through some kind of networking in which younger parents can benefit from the wisdom of others a few steps ahead. You can even make this a specialty network by bringing in people from various fields (e.g., a pediatrician to speak about nutrition and young people; a school coach to talk about teen fitness, etc.) who also have hearts for God. Again, these may be within your congregation or another church, but such collective wisdom can help you reach your goal of developing kids who love God with all their hearts, souls, minds, and strength.

HELP TEENS NOTICE MENTORING CONNECTIONS

As one committed to building strong relationships with teens, you have a great opportunity to help them apply this principle in practical ways. For example, if you take a group of students on a retreat, don't make all the application centered on their own relationships with God; instead tell them that their first chance to apply everything they've learned is when their family picks them up or when they sit around the dinner table.

There's more to this step, though. Some kids won't respond well to any changes in their parents' lives if their parents have hurt them in the past. This can also be true of other adults. For instance, it can be awkward when a schoolteacher they don't get along with visits your congregation on a Sunday morning.

Helping students aspire to surrender doesn't mean all these issues go away just because you want them to. It means that everyone gets a clean slate, and young people have to be taught how to do this. By nature, they are inclined to consumerism and may not consider how their self-interests affect others. Perhaps this is why it's a big deal when they go out of their way to be a blessing instead.

The benefit of all this is truly what the Bible promises. Long after these young people have moved on from your youth ministry, they will continue to be linked in some way to their families. Helping them learn to appreciate their parents now will pave the way for healthier connections down the road.

ESTABLISH CREDIBILITY

As much as we want immediate respect from parents and other adults, we may have to earn it. The following are some intentional steps you can take to garner and increase a sense of cooperative support:

COMMUNICATE YOUR VISION FOR STUDENTS IN A BRIEF-YET-POWERFUL WAY

The more specific and intentional your words are, the better you can articulate your goals and help others get a grip on them, too. The classic advice[4] is to have a mission statement brief enough for the front of a T-shirt and complete enough that it doesn't need explanation.

OVER-COMMUNICATE

Yes, this idea is mentioned twice in this chapter on purpose. The more you help parents and other adults stay informed about the details of all that you're doing with youth, the more secure they'll feel about what you're doing, and why you're doing it.

BRAG ON EVERYONE BUT YOURSELF

Don't place yourself in the spotlight; instead give your best and encourage others who are doing the same.

BE AS PROFESSIONAL AS YOU'RE ABLE, EVEN WHEN YOU FEEL UNPROFESSIONAL

There will be times when people expect you to act as if you are a paid professional. While you aren't, don't let that hold you back from giving your best.

HONOR TIME COMMITMENTS

When you say you'll be back from a trip at a certain hour, plan to be there a bit earlier. Honor whatever calendar you distribute (with rare cancellations and changes) and return phone calls within a reasonable amount of time.

---

4. Often attributed to leadership guru Peter Drucker.

CREATE FINANCIAL ACCOUNTABILITY

There will be times when you have to handle finances for trips and budget fundraisers. Keep a good paper trail and don't overspend.

BE READY FOR SKEPTICISM

There is a discussion you will have with a great number of parents and adults you encounter regarding religion. Perhaps they grew up with a negative concept of God and the church. They've since developed a philosophy that affects the way they parent their own children with regard to God and church, and it's "the talk" that will likely come up with you.

All of these steps can add to the trustworthiness you hope to establish with others. By practicing all of these little things in decent ways, you'll pave the way for more significant conversations to happen.

CHAPTER 8

WORKING WITH OTHER CHURCHES

One mark of a healthy ministry is its willingness to work with other movements of God, resulting in greater spiritual opportunities to impact people in our communities, including a growing appreciation and respect for what each group brings to the table. It's as if we've all gathered around the same cross of Christ, only from different angles that cause us to see and appreciate certain pieces of God's identity over another. Sharing our "perspectives" better completes the spiritual puzzle we're all attempting to form.

Some ministries never make it to that step, though. For among many churches there exists a suspicion and apprehension of "intermingling." Many congregations create policies that keep their ministries from working with other area churches, mainly out of fear of losing their church's personal and biblical integrity. While each would affirm the desire to work together for the sake of the people we're all trying to reach, each might also confess, "It's just easier to do it on our own."

WHY EVEN CONSIDER NETWORKING?

If you've ever tried working with other churches over a period of time, you'll eventually hear or ask the question, "Is it worth it?" Part of why that question is asked is due to how much work is involved in figuring out what's essential and nonessential to a cooperative association.

I've been part of meetings during which it seemed as though the only agenda was "Don't offend," and then there have been other occasions when the goal was "Let's win this city to Jesus Christ!" Both take tremendous patience and prayer to navigate, but one is clearly different than the other in that it is *for* something instead of merely *avoiding* something.

Yet there remain some very good reasons why you should face these hurdles with a smile on your face:

YOUR CHURCH IS PART OF *THE CHURCH*

Working with other churches is like taking part in a family reunion. Attending the party doesn't negate your household, but it offers a context within the greater family tree. It also helps you appreciate sights, sounds, tastes, smells, and sensations that bring out new ideas and practices to your usual routine.

> Starting from the beginning, Peter told them the whole story: "I was in the city of Joppa praying, and in a trance I saw a vision. I saw something like a large sheet being let down from heaven by its four corners, and it came down to where I was. I looked into it and saw four-footed animals of the earth, wild beasts, reptiles, and birds of the air. Then I heard a voice telling me, 'Get up, Peter. Kill and eat.'
>
> I replied, "Surely not, Lord! Nothing impure or unclean has ever entered my mouth."
>
> The voice spoke from heaven a second time, "Do not call anything impure that God has made clean." This happened three times, and then it was all pulled up to heaven again."
>
> (Acts 11:4-10)

The rest of the world doesn't see things as separated like we Christians do. Think about this for a moment: *We make more separations within the church than the world does!* As they look at us, they don't see "Methodist" or "Baptist"—they simply see "the church." Might the "foolish things" of this world be able to shame "the wise" into unity? (1 Corinthians 1:27)

> May the God who gives endurance and encouragement give you the same attitude of mind toward each other that Christ Jesus had, so that with one mind and one voice you may glorify the God and Father of our Lord Jesus Christ. Accept one another, then, just as Christ accepted you, in order to bring praise to God ... and ... that the Gentiles may glorify God for his mercy.
>
> (Romans 15:5-7; 9)

You can't do it alone. No matter what size your ministry is, you simply can't accomplish everything on your own. You'll tell the difference, too, if your goal is to build the biggest show in town versus reaching the young people in your community. Let the mission become greater than your own self-minded interests, and you will easily find yourself working alongside others with the same heart.

> "But seek first his kingdom and his righteousness, and all these things will be given to you as well."
>
> (Matthew 6:33)

It's a glimpse of heaven. Once heaven and earth collide together in the final restoration of things, there won't be all these divisions and denominations. There will simply be those who are with God and those who are not. May we pray and act in the direction of God's kingdom coming, that his will be done "on earth as it is in heaven" (Matthew 6:10).

> "After this I looked, and there before me was a great multitude that no one could count, from every nation, tribe, people and language, standing before the throne and before the Lamb. They were wearing white robes and were holding palm branches in their hands."
>
> (Revelation 7:9)

SOME THINGS TO CONSIDER

As previously mentioned, there's a perceived risk in working with other churches. Though many churches may not admit it, there's often an underlying fear that a family might leave your congregation if what's being offered across town has more appeal to the student. Most church leaders will recognize this concern, confess it, and allow God to guide them in a healthy way. Others, though, can sometimes let this fear get to them and prevent valuable ministry from taking place.

On the other hand, just because you can connect with other churches doesn't mean you should do so blindly. As you deal with other ministries with future events and activities, consider the following list of topics to address:

THE PRAYER AND PLANNING PROCESS

Prayer is a value everyone agrees on and yet is often approached with a sense of obligation more than desperation. It can ultimately destroy ego and arrogance in leaders, allowing the planning process to go much more smoothly. Both prayer and planning should take place well in advance of your actual event and include great measures of space and grace.

While prayer can truly create unity, there's also the ironic matter of making it happen beyond personal preferences. In some prayer meetings the question can become "How do we pray?" or "Should we pray this or that?" This is the first opportunity we have to settle how we will regard one another and whether or not our usual approach to intercession is as important as we think.

THE GOAL OF THE EVENT

Generally speaking, the more relational your event is the easier it's going to be to work with another church. When you turn the corner into more spiritual applications, though, the style and theology of each ministry may begin to become an issue. For instance, an outreach event is an amazing opportunity for churches to work together, but how you invite students to Christ—and who can effectively present such an invitation—must be discussed with humility and tact.

Some common ways to get together with other ministries involve service. It's hard to disagree about whether or not to serve the poor or invest resources together for the sake of blessing your region. This can be an activity in and of itself, or it can take another step through evangelistic prayer.

THE ADULT LEADERSHIP TEAM

Work hard to create a sense of "one adult leadership team" versus several individual teams from the various ministries. Simple efforts such as wearing the same T-shirt or having similar hanging name badges go a long way, as well as getting everyone together before the event for prayer. Buddy up leaders with other adults from outside their own ministries, allowing the pairs to effectively minister to more students at once.

A word of caution: Your ministry may have higher standards about who can be an adult leader than other churches do. Sometimes it's seen in age as some youth groups allow college-age young adults to be leaders over high school students, while others may not allow such close age proximity. Other times it can be a matter of what's considered "freedom" versus "sin," and so if one adult heads to the parking lot for a smoking break, it might cause another to feel a line has been crossed. Handle such matters ahead of time, creating a temporary policy for the event that can serve everyone in the long run.

THE STUDENTS WHO ATTEND

At any event, there are students you expect to come and those whose presence is something of a surprise. Young people sometimes feel more comfortable coming to activities if they have a guaranteed friend, and so you may have the chance to interact with a circle of your students' relationships you may otherwise not see. There also may be teenagers who show up with the wrong motives, looking to kill boredom or take advantage of what you're offering. But if your adult leaders are sharp and working well together, all of these issues can be tactfully addressed.

THE FOLLOW-UP

If your activity is for the students already in your ministry, follow-up may also be a relatively easy matter. But if new students take part, someone should follow up with them on behalf of the event. To do this without seeming as though one church is trying to lay claim can become a touchy issue. Again, though, if a humble spirit is already in place this shouldn't be much of a hurdle. One suggestion is to send a general postcard with each ministry's info on it to everyone.

CONSIDER THE FUTURE

Once you've done the work of creating a climate of prayer and affinity, you're ready to do more than host one successful cross-church event. As God leads you, consider a "loose" relationship with area ministries that inspires major Christ-centered unity instead of exaggerating minor differences. You'll want to be sure this helps your ministry's specific calling in your community, for this will give you a sense of peace if things become chaotic.

Another thing to take into account with your partnerships is how they must transcend a personal friendship. There is a unique turnover in youth ministry that moves leaders around more than they'd like. While you may have a great friendship with a youth worker in another ministry, be sure you're building something that transcends your current relationship. The size of your congregation and theirs can make a difference in how easily this occurs, so start early.

Along these lines, consider worshiping with the other church before the event. Too often we visit other churches only when looking for a new one to join. Every worship experience and style can broaden your perspective on the many creative ways to worship God. You'll not only deepen your sense of connection to your spiritual brothers and sisters, but also you can uncover God through moments of silence and breathtaking praise simply because you're not used to them—all of which has the power to draw students and yourself closer to God.

In other words, do whatever you can to keep the focus on what matters most. And if you need to connect with others outside your circle to do it, be sure to do it. Remember, God's ultimate intention for us is not that we connect with other churches to feel good about ourselves; the whole point in getting together is so God can have a greater impact on us...which in turn creates a greater impact on our communities.

CHAPTER 9

WORKING WITH SCHOOLS AND OTHER SOCIAL ORGANIZATIONS

A teenage guy had asked to use my phone, hoping to call the local high school football coach. Since he and I had discussed the topic at hand for a few weeks, I observed the conversation unfold in front of me—and I felt as though a great victory was taking place.

In hindsight, though, I wish I could go back and correct all of the things that went down.

The guy was about to become a high school freshman in a rural community with an unusually high commitment to athletics. It almost seemed like a rite of passage for a guy to go out for the football team, and I had grown to resent the way school sports had become a kind of acceptable idol the local households endorsed. As a youth worker I often had to deal with halfhearted commitment to our meetings and events as a result—especially the year that all but three students in the entire junior high went out for the track team.

So imagine my surprise when this student called up his coach to tell him he wasn't going to play football that season.

"Coach," he said, "I won't be on the team this year. I'm going to be spending my time at church instead." You have to understand that hearing those words come out of his mouth in that town was akin to an NFL player giving up a season (and a huge paycheck) because of his faith.

Keep in mind I never preached against the athletic program out loud. I tactfully spoke of "praying about all your commitments, being sure you were spending your time as God wanted you to." Beneath the surface, though, I was tired of our youth group being in constant competition with the sports schedule, not to mention the way the school seemed to propagate it further all the time.

As I listened to the student's side of the phone conversation, I felt like it was God's way of affirming me for my challenges. I imagined that it was the beginning of a small revolution that not only would transform the town but also give me value as a youth worker—after all, getting kids to choose youth group over anything else is the most important priority, right?

ANOTHER PERSPECTIVE

All throughout the year following that conversation, that student had a strong commitment to our youth group. He gave up football as well as other extracurricular opportunities, all so he could take some steps forward in his relationship with Jesus Christ. He and I also bonded relationally, and we enjoyed a great time of mentoring.

But the "revolution" didn't pan out like I thought it would. In fact, I ended up moving away from that church the next year. Consequently, the student lost his groove with the church, joined the football team, and got into a spiral of bad decisions that tracked back to the group of guys he played with. This only seemed to affirm my beliefs about the whole matter.

That is, until a short time after my move when I sat down with a mentor of mine. I thought sharing this tale of "success" and "failure" would help him to see me as an effective youth worker, so I told him the whole story with a sense of my own self-importance. After I finished the summary, he pulled back a bit from the restaurant table and chose his words with great wisdom.

"So you were mentoring him?" he asked. "Yes," I answered. "We spent a lot of time together, and he was very receptive to my guidance."

"Just a thought," he replied. "What if he was supposed to play football and change things from the inside out?"

I paused. "What do you mean?"

He continued. "Did you ever consider your role as a youth worker in his life was to help him become an evangelist to his friends? Maybe even his teammates?"

"Well," I stumbled, "that's what our youth group was for." Even as I said it, I knew this was an incomplete thought.

"Hmm," he said. "I always thought God liked to work in more than one place. Seems like a school is just as good a place as any, don't you think?"

THE LOCAL MISSION FIELD

Let's clarify the point: The local school, sports programs, band/orchestra, arts course, and so on, are not your enemies. There are also many community organizations that are equally not against you, from local 4-H competitions to the Boy Scouts, Girl Scouts, karate classes, and so on. While the schedule and demands of each of these may run against the grain of your ministry endeavors, they're all completely neutral media that become subjective only when certain voices or agendas rise to the surface. This means that if we truly believe that God is already at work in all places, then the question becomes if we will help nurture a revelation of his presence within those environments or merely struggle against them.

Take into account the various people a local campus or social organization will affect:

Young people: For the short, concentrated time students walk the hallways of their middle schools or high schools, they will spend the majority of their hours each week within them. Likewise, many of the events happening in a region are often centered around young people.

Parents/extended family: With all extracurricular activities, parents and family members are invited to cheer on participating students. This means yet another chance to make an investment in them.

Faculty: Teachers, school administrators, and other staff are more than the duties they perform within a school building; they're also everyday people with real issues they're trying to sort out. It's easy to forget this, though, as we often view community instructors, referees, and so on as one-dimensional people.

The community: Drawn by in-house theatrical and music productions or local athletics that become the talk of the town, the people who live around the school often enjoy stepping onto campus. Perfect strangers can become familiar faces at events, soon becoming fans of the teens taking part.

Considering these various people groups, might there be an opportunity for your ministry to uniquely affect the spiritual climate of a school or social organization in a powerfully positive way? Right now there are Christians and not-yet-Christians in every one of these aforementioned roles, each needing a special kind of encouragement and challenge. With a majority of teenagers feeling disconnected from God and church, we must take to heart what it means to be the church to them. Jesus said, *"Go into all the world and preach the gospel to all creation"* (Mark 16:15), which means we have to do just that—*GO*.

You and the Christian community you serve are uniquely in place for this very reason. While you may have a distinctively Christian environment set up for meeting with your students, the story doesn't end there. Keeping in mind the influence that classes, teams, bands, clubs, and general social circles can have on teenagers, someone needs to take seriously the call to influence those networks.

THINKING LIKE A MISSIONARY

Most people understand a missionary as someone who crosses a cultural line in order to introduce people to Jesus Christ. This definition transcends the usual context of foreign countries, though. Every time you leave the comfort of your familiar adult or Christian environments in order to impact the youth and mainstream "cultures" with the Good News, you're as much of a missionary as if you'd crossed a geographical border.

Jesus Christ modeled this for us, leaving the glory of his place in heaven to spend time with humans who were far from God. He knew what it meant to be rejected, too; for as much as he became flesh and dwelt among us, many rejected him and misunderstood his motives. (John 1:1, 10-11, 12, 14) Meaning we should feel no surprise when we encounter similar resistance to our endeavors. You're not alone in what you're attempting to accomplish within your local schools—because Jesus is already at work in the hearts of everyone concerned. In fact, God is the one who put that very vision into you in the first place.

Recognizing this can help you become spiritually alert to whatever the Holy Spirit is up to on a campus. The best places to look are the varying circles of relationships to which you have a special proximity, whether they're students you know in some way or faculty with whom you share interests. Just as a missionary must establish a core network of support and outreach, so must you seek God to gain insights about the individuals God wants you to reach with him.

In fact, this bite-sized approach may very well save you from feeling overwhelmed at the task ahead of you. As a volunteer youth worker, you may feel it's not even worth trying to crack the campus since the time, effort, and resistance seem so impossible to attempt. Take heart, for while you aren't alone with God by your side, you also aren't alone in this endeavor—other churches dream about the same end goal, too.

I've found that while one church in town may effectively reach a school's artistic participants, another may find the academic or athletic side easier to connect with. Recognizing this will allow you to worry less about who you aren't reaching and stay focused and encouraged about who you *are* reaching.

Like missionaries, find a way into schools' cultures that allows you to naturally "do what they do" without losing your identity in the process. Simply enjoy and accept them, affirming what's good about their values and feeling out how to share the story of Jesus in their "language." If you're going to invite them to follow him, you'll want to be sure you're using their terminologies in an accurate way and not merely your church's words in a religious sense.

Wisdom from the Trenches

One of the greatest partnerships that can be established for a youth worker or a local youth ministry is with the area school systems. These mission fields embody the people and ideologies our churches are trying to reach and connect with, so it only makes sense that establishing a solid relationship with them is critical.

At times, though, it's tricky. While the leadership in many school systems are aware of and grateful for what youth ministries try to do, many nevertheless believe that the relationship needs to stay at arm's length. Fortunately, in my context, I've been able to build some solid relationships with the school leadership. This has translated into the school opening its doors to me and allowing me the chance to be very involved without much red tape. Over the years I've been able to offer counsel when there's been a death or crisis in the school; I've also been able to play a significant role in bringing in guest speakers or helping organize the school's baccalaureate service.

It's rewarding to walk through the school, travel around town, or attend an athletic event and have the principal, a teacher, or a guidance counselor say hello and call me out by name. I believe this connection happens because the relationship between our youth ministry and the school is rooted in respect and communication. I've found that the more you're willing to honor the core desires of the school, the more room you have to communicate your goals, desires, and wishes. It's a great foundation to build on, and I'm extremely thankful for the way I've seen this play out with our local school system and youth ministry.

—Jeff Luedtke, youth worker for 14 years

A FEW HURDLES

A growing trend among schools and social organizations in America is the increased demand of teenagers' time. Young people are getting up earlier for "zero hour" class periods after they've stayed up late to complete all their homework, practices, and projects. To top it off, most schools and groups no longer consider "Sabbath days" when it comes to scheduling events. Youth groups used to meet on Wednesdays and Sundays, confident that the local community wouldn't schedule anything to compete for that slot. But these days most any time slot seems like fair game.

This is more than a school-year issue, though; even in the summer there are academic study groups, athletic camps, stage productions, and so on that draw students into routines that are just as busy. Since teenagers are often reluctant to take part in special trips unless they know peers who're attending, you may find it valuable during the planning stages to consider the schedules of some of your more influential students, since their presence may inspire others to take part. That's not to say these teens are more important than others, but their absence or participation may create the most indigenous ripples.

Beyond the matter of time, there's also the challenge of presence. Several steps have been taken in recent decades to give students the right to hold religious meetings and prayer clubs on school campuses. The Equal Access Act is perhaps the most noteworthy, signed into law by President Reagan in 1984. It allows teenagers to initiate gatherings with a limited open forum, permitting various adults on campus upon invitation. Most schools encourage or require an adult staff liaison to the students, but even he/she is there in a nonparticipatory capacity.

Another key matter to confront is the spiritual temperament of the administration and faculty. I've witnessed what happens when teachers, principals, and coaches love Jesus Christ and allow him to shine through their lives. Likewise I've witnessed the negative impact of those who are apathetic or antagonistic toward spiritual matters, especially upon students. While all teachers must maintain objectivity, some are more willing to work with you and your ministry than others. Praying through that journey and discerning whom to approach is more important than we may realize.

Finally, don't forget that God's enemy is working on the campus and in each of these organizations, too. He's quite crafty and has been using some of the same tricks and traps to steal, kill, and destroy young people today that he did years ago. Don't ever assume you're wrestling against only the flesh and blood of the school system, but be fully equipped with God's armor as you confront the rulers and principalities of darkness that are more real than we realize.

SOME STEPS YOU CAN TAKE

While it may seem at times as though the deck is stacked against you, there are some very simple principles you can follow to penetrate a campus in the name of Jesus:

PRAY FOR THE SCHOOL

While this is first on this list, for some reason it's the step many of us neglect. Prayer enlarges your perspective for the school, seeing it through the eyes of God with an understanding of his heart and strength to accomplish its redemption. When you carve out such a priority through sacrificial time and heartfelt focus, you position yourself and those around you—quite possibly even a whole campus—to better respond to God like a sail responds to the wind.

And obviously this is bigger than your own personal prayers for the school. Work hard to develop prayer networks with other youth workers and the students on campus. In one church for which I served, a group of students from various congregations met for a five-minute prayer time before school each day. They found it a great way to acknowledge themselves before God and each other, reminding them of their mission on earth. All that year their "spiritual antennas" were better raised to whatever the Holy Spirit was doing all around them.

> Also, seek the peace and prosperity of the city to which I have carried you into exile. Pray to the LORD for it, because if it prospers, you too will prosper.
>
> (Jeremiah 29:7)

IDEAS

- Initiate a monthly prayer breakfast where teens gather to pray together before school;

- Go through the yearbook and encourage your church to "adopt a page" to pray for those students/teachers for a week;
- Use a calendar to create a schedule of key moments for you and the students to pray for each other (e.g., tests, social events, faith sharing opportunities, etc.);
- Help coordinate special prayer gatherings with other churches around special events and holidays (e.g., See You at the Pole; first day of school; National Day of Prayer, etc).

VISIT THE SCHOOL

One intriguing aspect of Jesus' ministry is that his capacity to do ministry and perform miracles often related directly to how much people trusted him. Perhaps this is why you should really consider finding a natural, unforced way onto the campus, since most schools already question your motives. You don't want to come across as a salesman but as someone with a vested interest in the school. Intentionally connect with key leaders to help them know who you are so that they might have greater confidence in whatever ministry you're attempting.

One way I enjoyed connecting with the school was through volunteering at the football concession stand at home games. This allowed me the chance to see students I already knew, but it also let me meet their friends, parents, and teachers. Another successful move was always introducing myself to the principal and asking how I might serve his/her agenda for the school. This was all new territory for me, but my outreach capacity enlarged as I became a recognizable face around the campus. You never know how one awkward, risky step can strengthen future ones.

The Word became flesh and made his dwelling among us.

(John 1:14)

IDEAS

- Bring lunch to the campus, whether it's for your students and their friends or the office staff;
- Volunteer your time to tutor kids;
- Bring donuts to the office staff once a week;
- Create high-quality T-shirts for kids to wear to school;
- Get permission from parents to give their kids rides home;
- Send notes of appreciation to the faculty;
- Substitute teach;

- Create "back to school" packs of encouragement, each with a note that says, "We're here for you and want you to have an amazing year. Let us know how we can serve you at any time."

UNDERSTAND THE SCHOOL

Every school values something, and often the school becomes known for that value. Maybe the value (like the school I mentioned at the beginning of this chapter) is athletics; maybe it's something more academic. Some schools pride themselves on their facilities while others enjoy high moral codes of conduct. The point is that whatever the value is, aim to understand it and not resent it. It truly can work in your favor to understand the personality of your school, especially if you find a way to use its thoughts and questions to connect people with God.

You don't have to go at this alone, though. Use the natural environments of a community to interact with people, listen to comments, and study the presentation of the literature. Arrive early to activities and leave late, observing what the kids do in each situation, who they sit with, how they pass the time in awkward moments—and any link they have with adults during it all. Develop a set of friendly questions you can use to dialogue with students, teachers, and parents about their perceptions of things.

> Paul then stood up in the meeting of the Areopagus and said: "Men of Athens! I see that in every way you are very religious. For as I walked around and looked carefully at your objects of worship, I even found an altar with this inscription: TO AN UNKNOWN GOD. So you are of the very thing you worship—and this is what I am going to proclaim to you."
>
> (Acts 17:22-23)

IDEAS

- Attend PTA meetings;
- Attend sporting events, using game time to walk around the stands;
- Buy advertising space in the school newspaper;
- Invite Christian teachers/staff to speak at your youth meetings;
- Practice learning names and using them to ask people of all ages how they're doing.

SERVE THE SCHOOL

You know those jobs around your house that no one likes to do? Schools have those tasks, too. So when you humble yourself and step into the gap to get them done, people notice. I once built a great relationship with a district athletic director who appreciated our youth group cleaning up dropped food, candy, and drinks under the bleachers after football games. We supplied the manpower needed to accomplish something that needed to be done but hardly anyone would volunteer to do.

Keep in mind that there's something you're good at that can be your way of serving a campus. Maybe you have a background in a sport that would allow you the chance to help a coaching staff. Perhaps you have administrative skills that you can volunteer to the school office. Even your time is a resource, from volunteering to chaperone trips to keeping an eye on the cafeteria during lunch.

Imagine what would happen to the authority and sincerity of your message if you were viewed as someone who served the greater interests of God and the school at the same time. Might not more people be intrigued at your selfless attitude and perhaps reform their definition of *Christian*? Just as missionaries work to share eternal truths in an understandable language, serving is a universal "tongue" that will help you share the good news of Jesus in a relevant way.

> This, then, is how you ought to regard us: as servants of Christ and as those entrusted with the mysteries God has revealed.
>
> (1 Corinthians 4:1)

IDEAS

- Invite the school to use your church facilities for everything from athletic gatherings and concerts to debates and study groups;
- Host a graduation ceremony honoring seniors;
- Volunteer to help set up during special events.

A BIT OF PRACTICAL THEOLOGY

Bear in mind that as a "missionary" you're in the midst of a powerful movement of God. Our challenge isn't to remove students from the world but to help them be restored back to God as he protects them from the evil one. (John 17:15) God's love for you, students, and faculty is incredible in that he hopes for "none to perish" (2 Peter 3:9). This is God's desire for everyone, so it's time for it to begin in you.

It's in your court to realize that you're called to do more than merely take care of the kids already in your church or youth ministry. In order to reach out and redemptively love all people into a deeper connection with God, your heart must first enlarge. Chances are that this won't happen unless you intentionally create opportunities for God to work in and through your life, so consider the various things you can do to make that happen.

One of the simplest ways this played out for me over the years was when I served as a substitute teacher in the school system I was nearest to. Each district has standards regarding whom they allow to sub, but even if you don't qualify, there's usually some opportunity to get on campus during school hours if you look for it. The insights you can gain during this window of an academic day may very well trump any you'd glean before or after it.

As a sub, I expected to encounter and get the chance to know nonchurched kids. Of course that did happen, and several connections were formed throughout that experience. What was most enlightening, though, was how the kids I already knew acted somewhat differently in their school environments as opposed to the church environment in which I was used to seeing them. Many whom I expected to enjoy seeing me on campus kept their distance, while others surprised me with their unashamed friendship in front of their peers.

Through that experience and others, I've learned how to help students better think through and pray through the social pressures found in most school environments and other social organizations. Even the Christian students whom we think we know best can succumb to the pressure to become people they aren't. If we're blind to this area simply because we don't enter it, we can't effectively guide these students to live integrated lives. Just consider how they spend so much time in school, and yet we often can spend so little.

Imagine what would happen if we decided to walk on campus in the power of the Holy Spirit to meet kids on their turf, in their time, and according to their terms. While these environments can feel hostile and pressure-packed, we could take the offense in the name of Jesus to reach youth right where they are. There wouldn't need to be any fear in what we were up to because we'd simply be joining God in what he's doing. God is the One who can transform a local school, and his hope is that we might share in this awesome process.

The campus environment often forces students to face a variety of emotional, social, and spiritual challenges, and the weight of these problems has become especially acute in recent years in public schools. Students need adults who care enough to relate to them where they are and offer a life-changing relationship with Jesus Christ. Be available and encouraging, taking your time to become a fellow traveler (and not merely a "travel agent").

Again, you certainly will encounter many students with whom you can share Jesus. However, you'll also find renewed connections with your own students, solid networking you can establish with the administration, and a Christ-fueled love for all people of all ages. For all you know, taking this step may be the very thing God uses to grow you up in your relationship with him—so if you don't go this route, you may miss an important faith step for you. Remember that God wants to transform others, *and God wants to transform you as well.*

CHAPTER 10

WORKING WITH INDIVIDUALS IN TIMES OF CRISIS

"I'm never getting married."

I looked up from my video camera when I heard this statement come out of the mouth of a girl in our youth group. I was a college-aged volunteer youth worker, hosting a breakfast at my house where the teen guys in our ministry cooked breakfast for the girls. In the midst of lighthearted conversation, this declaration seemed somewhat out of place.

"Why not?" I asked, still filming.

The girl was silent, averting her eyes from me and moving on to other topics. This only made things even more awkward, and I realized that the camera in my hand wasn't helping. I turned it off and set it down, moving to sit in a chair near her.

"I'm sorry," I said, "I didn't catch why you said what you said."

"I don't want to talk about it," she replied. "Can someone pass the syrup?"

And that was it. The conversation ended as quickly as it began; she shut down, and I didn't know how to respond. Everything I tried to do to further the dialogue only resulted in more resistance on her end and frustration on mine. I felt like I'd missed something important, and in doing so believed I failed as a youth worker. I hadn't, mind you, but I allowed my sense of identity to get wrapped up in how I couldn't fix what was wrong in a student (let alone figure out what the actual problem was).

A week later I learned that the girl's parents had recently told her they were getting a divorce. This is probably what prompted her to say what she did, especially in a moment when she felt relaxed and among friends. Of course I didn't get the information from her but from another student who came to me in a crisis because of this other girl's crisis.

Did you catch that? A crisis—and a crisis about that very same crisis—gave me a crisis about the crisis about the crisis, as well as one for the crisis that began it all.

Maybe you can relate, for the theme of this chapter is perhaps all too familiar. All around you are young people in various predicaments, from the unexpected short-term emergencies to the wearying long-term trials that won't go away anytime soon. Even if they haven't yet realized the full weight of what they're going through, youth feel the effects of crisis and are attempting to get out from under the pressure. But often they can't find the language to describe their feelings, adding to the already growing circumstantial stress.

To top it off, they often believe that nobody "gets" things the way they do. Ironically, you probably *do* get where they're coming from because it's easy for many youth workers to feel sympathy pains as they experience crises of their own. Because for every student who feels a loss of direction, there's often an adult youth worker who feels a similar confusion about how to respond. Our hearts ache for what we see them experiencing, and yet our lack of words or wisdom can make us feel ineffective...even though we really aren't.

So take hope—there's a practical direction for you and for them that can turn today's blindness into tomorrow's hindsight.

TURN YOUR EYES UPON JESUS

This will be difficult for many people, and you'll need to take a good look in the mirror under the guidance of the Holy Spirit to ask how it applies to you. So get out your highlighter or pen and make a lot of marks around what you're about to read.

The only way you can truly help young people in crisis is when you realize you haven't been called to become their Savior but to point them to the One who is.

Before you dismiss that idea as something you already know, please reread it and reconsider what it means in a practical sense. This declaration is calling you to give up your desire to receive gratitude from the teens who may come your way, thanking you for "being there" in the hard times. It's not that you don't deserve it, for my guess is that you're reading this book because you love young people and very much *do* deserve thanks. Knowing that, though, I'd warn you that your presence in a crisis is meant primarily to build a bridge to God—not merely to you.

In pointing this out, I don't mean to imply that your motives aren't pure in any way. I've watched many amazing youth workers go in with the greatest of intentions when crises hit students they care about. In many cases, though, lines get blurred and soon ministry done in the name of Jesus becomes all about your ministry and less about Jesus. If you're not careful, you might enjoy feeling needed so much that you actually move from one crisis to the next, seeking your worth in reactive care versus proactive investment.

Consider how Jesus separated his miracles from his ministry. The following occurred after Jesus fed more than 5,000 followers and healed many sick people:

> Once the crowd realized that neither Jesus nor his disciples were there, they got into the boats and went to Capernaum in search of Jesus. When they found him on the other side of the lake, they asked him, "Rabbi, when did you get here?"

> Jesus answered, "Very truly I tell you, you are looking for me, not because you saw the signs I performed but because you ate the loaves and had your fill. Do not work for food that spoils, but for food that endures to eternal life, which the Son of Man will give you. For on him God the Father has placed his seal of approval."

> (John 6:24-27)

The most immediate thing a young person in crisis wants is the healing to begin. This may very well be your heart, too, but at times the desire for the miracle can get in the way of the mission God is after. If you can turn your eyes on Jesus, you will better be able to help kids in crisis do the same.

And that's where the true healing begins.

Wisdom from the Trenches

The biggest piece of advice I could ever give to a volunteer youth worker is to build healthy boundaries. Too often I've met volunteers who've said "yes" to the youth group and had their lives taken over. Instead dedicate yourself to fully helping in a couple of areas and politely decline the rest. You can't be there for everyone, nor should you try to be. This will help you avoid the dreaded volunteer burnout.

—*Adam McClane, youth worker*

TURN THEIR EYES UPON JESUS

The task of helping students focus on God during a crisis doesn't mean we make them ignore the storm but rather recognize the greater perspective of it. Do this correctly, and you'll help them develop the ability to trust God in any future pressures they face. If you don't believe you can effectively do this, though, you're in good company.

> That day when evening came, he said to his disciples, "Let us go over to the other side." Leaving the crowd behind, they took him along, just as he was, in the boat. There were also other boats with him. A furious squall came up, and the waves broke over the boat, so that it was nearly swamped. Jesus was in the stern, sleeping on a cushion. The disciples woke him and said to him, "Teacher, don't you care if we drown?"
>
> He got up, rebuked the wind and said to the waves, "Quiet! Be still!" Then the wind died down and it was completely calm.
>
> He said to his disciples, "Why are you so afraid? Do you still have no faith?"
>
> They were terrified and asked each other, "Who is this? Even the wind and the waves obey him!"
>
> (Mark 4:35-41)

I hope you find encouragement in this passage, for even Jesus dealt with distracted disciples who chose to put their eyes on the storm instead of on him. There's also a rather intriguing insight these verses provide regarding what a crisis is and what a crisis isn't. While the disciples panicked over the intensity of the waves and rain, Jesus rested himself on a cushion.

A CUSHION

There is more to that piece of Scripture than mere information. Just as Jesus rested during a storm, so are you called to—and able to—enter a teenager's raging chaos with peace that passes all understanding. (Philippians 4:7) This "cushion" you rest upon is a fruit of the Spirit, partnering with love, joy, patience, goodness, kindness, gentleness, faithfulness, and self-control—available in every situation. (Galatians 5:22-23) Allowing God to place that fruit in your life will help you better discern the crisis with a clearer perspective.

IT IS/ISN'T A BIG DEAL

Take a look at these statements and decide which of them you consider a crisis compared to what students might think:

- Sara is pregnant and her parents don't know.
- Phil and his dad were heading to their car after a sporting event when someone held them up at gunpoint.
- Mary can't find her cell phone.
- Jimmy can't seem to please his boss at the movie theater where he works part-time as an usher.
- Anna can't shake her headache.
- Rick has a dentist appointment on Friday.
- Vanessa's car is low on gas.

What was easy or difficult about this exercise? Chances are a few may have seemed easy to identify as a crisis while others weren't quite as clear. What if "Sara" is a dog? How about if the person who held up "Phil" at gunpoint was his little brother using a play gun? A lost cell phone may seem quite common, but what if "Mary" is walking down a dark street and thinks she's being followed?

You may already get the point, but it's worth stating that what seems like a crisis to some may look like "it's all in their head" to another. Let's say, for example, that "Jimmy's" issue is just as it reads, which is either small if you view it through the lens of "it's just a part-time job" or large if you understand that losing his job will only give his dad another reason to harshly criticize him. A headache may just be a headache, unless "Anna" is in the middle of taking her SATs for the final time to try to bring up her score so she can get into that college. And who knows what "Rick" and "Vanessa" are going through or if their situations are everyday matters or critical emergencies?

DO YOU SEE WHAT I SEE?

Personally speaking, every young person I've ever known has gone through some form of "crisis." That may seem like an overstatement, but a "crisis" to teenagers is more than something that makes national headlines. Teens tend to determine things more intrinsically and subjectively, and telling them that something isn't a big deal only aggravates the problem. Even if similar experiences have happened before, each person and circumstance is unique.

So we have to be careful to not project our assumptions and values on adolescents who are just starting to understand theirs. This means it's in our court to identify the details of each episode at play, striving for a perspective that's bigger than the pure emotions of the moment. Consider these elements present in most predicaments and the unique contributions they make to how things roll forward:

THE STUDENT WITH THE PROBLEM

You may be dealing with a young person who normally is quite confident but now is suddenly flustered—or find the opposite to be true. Each kid is different, not just from each other but even to themselves. You can't expect students to respond the same way today that they responded in the past, so approach crises understanding that who they are now may not be part of their permanent identities.

Questions:

- Would you describe them as solid in the faith or spiritually shaky?
- Do the youth know how to transform feelings into productive words and actions or will they need some coaching in that area?
- How open are they to anything practical you or God might offer?
- Is there a sense that the situation is creating a lasting dent on their understandings of their identities?

THE PERSON/PEOPLE THE STUDENT HAS THE PROBLEM WITH

Some people with whom students have crises possess large voices in the process of determining how things play out. In some cases, these people control their own voices; but in most instances, these people have only as much power as the youths in crisis allow them to have.

Questions:

- Is this individual or group of people open to resolution?
- Does the student feel ready and able to speak to this person/these people?
- What grip will this person or these people have on the student in the future if things remain unresolved?

THE TIMING OF THE PROBLEM

Oddly enough, some issues won't seem as chaotic as others based solely on timing. For instance, not having a date for Friday night normally isn't a big deal; but if this particular Friday is a big school dance, the timing magnifies the issue.

Questions:

- When did the situation occur, and what was the young person doing when it occurred?
- Is there a deadline for when this problem must be solved?
- If so, how clear is that timeline to the student?
- Was the moment everything happened expected or unexpected?

THE CONTEXT OF THE PROBLEM

Even seemingly familiar situations that the student has dealt with before are distinctly new, for each new situation contains factors that make it highly unique. Helping the student dig beneath the surface of an issue can help determine what truly occurred, why it happened, and the best approach to proactively moving forward.

Questions:

- Is this the first time the student has experienced this issue or the 50th?
- Where did it occur this time, and how did that play into things?
- Out of all the factors at play, which is the young person concentrating on the most and why?

THE SCOPE OF THE PROBLEM

Much like a pebble in a pond, there are things at play that this issue can affect over the long haul. Similarly, the very fact that it's affecting the student may be because the problem originally impacted someone else, and the teen got caught up in its wake.

Questions:

- Did this all happen from the outside in or from the inside out?
- How will the manner in which this is handled affect others?
- Does this crisis have the potential to permanently mark this teenager in a negative way?

THE PRESENT OF PRESENCE

Entering into the details of crises with students doesn't mean you shouldn't offer an enlarged perspective, though. In what you say and what you do, try to keep a balance that conveys to them God's unending presence and ability to turn backward situations into forward momentum. This may initially mean walking through their problems with them in supportive silence, but there is a time to establish a biblical foundation that offers them a greater point of view.

> Then the disciples went back to where they were staying. Now Mary stood outside the tomb crying. As she wept, she bent over to look into the tomb and saw two angels in white, seated where Jesus' body had been, one at the head and the other at the foot.
>
> They asked her, "Woman, why are you crying?"
>
> "They have taken my Lord away," she said, "and I don't know where they have put him." At this, she turned around and saw Jesus standing there, but she did not realize that it was Jesus.
>
> He asked her, "Women, why are you crying? Who is it you are looking for?"
>
> Thinking he was the gardener, she said, "Sir, if you have carried him away, tell me where you have put him, and I will get him."
>
> Jesus said to her, "Mary."
>
> She turned toward him and cried out in Aramaic, "Rabboni!" (which means Teacher).
>
> (John 20:10-16)

In this passage we see that Mary's sorrow and loss blinded her to the hope that was right in front of her. First Jesus tried to gain her attention through angels, and then Jesus himself began a conversation with her. Her weeping blurred her attention until she heard the voice of God speak her name.

There's a great takeaway here for all of us as we work with students. Just as Mary's emotions kept her from recognizing God, many teenagers in a crisis may emotionally react with misplaced cynicism that God will work in their lives. This isn't the time to debate theology, but instead to help them see that even when life hurts, God can heal.

How you do this will require discernment, for everyone reacts and grieves differently. Some young people may best respond to words of encouragement while others will draw great strength through an affirming pat on the back. Everything from the past factors in for teens, too, including whether this is their first big crisis event or if they've dealt with similar stress before.

There's no single formula for helping youth in crisis, but some wise words from James 1:19 remind us to "be quick to listen, slow to speak and slow to become angry." The more you are fully present and paying attention to the problem, the greater an impact you'll have when you do speak. Remember, the goal isn't to provide advice but to create appropriate reflection that leads young people to Jesus.

COMMON LANGUAGE

When the Twin Towers fell on September 11, 2001, many of the students I worked with at the time didn't have the vocabulary to describe their concept of the world. What they did have in common, though, was how everyone else in their relational circle shared the crisis. The continual coverage on television may have furthered the pain, but it also helped create a language for them to articulate what had occurred. Never in my life have I heard the word *surreal* used so often.

There are other times, though, that a crisis is local. It may be a situation that only a few people know about, so entering it may be difficult for you. Even if you normally have a close relationship with the student in crisis, you're now essentially an outsider and must be invited in. This is true in each of these possible crisis scenarios:

Personal crisis: "I'm going through something with myself."
Examples: Substance addiction; sexual habits; puberty; medical issues; identity issues.

Household crisis: "I'm going through something with my family."
Examples: Being compared to siblings; divorce; financial challenges; lost pet; lack of time with mom/dad; death in family.

Peer crisis: "I'm going through something with others my age."
Examples: Bullying at school; feeling out of place; others seem to be smarter or more skilled; argument with friends.

Geographical crisis: "I'm going through something with my world."
Examples: Jobs unavailable locally; global issues feeling close to home; school closing; neighborhood feels unsafe; etc.

Spiritual crisis: "I'm going through something with my God."
Examples: Lost a relational connection with church or youth ministry; initial emotions of coming to Jesus have "worn off"; unable to figure out what the next step of growth is; etc.

Even if you can see each of these situations clearly, your "outsider" status may invoke atypical behavior from students when you're around. For example, some students who are known for their gift of gab may become strangely quiet, while others who are normally quiet may try on new identities to distract themselves from the lives they're uncomfortable with. It's quite common during hard circumstances for teenagers to gather with friends and create the freedom to cry on each other's shoulders.

This is why the church was created to begin with—students, too, need to be surrounded by the body of Christ. When they feel a disconnection to God's goodness, your simple presence serves as a reminder that God does love them and hasn't gone anywhere. God alone can allow true healing to take place, for without him the aforementioned coping mechanisms will provide only a temporary fix. It's likely that even after students have said, "I'm fine now," they will reflect on major crisis events for the rest of their lives. Without the Holy Spirit being invited in now, they may not be in tune with him later.

GROWING UP BY FEELING DOWN

A crisis is not inherently negative, but an opportunity for a response. In every unique situation, there is one constant: Students need to take their struggles before the living God. The more honest they can become with him about what they're feeling, the more they can experience healing that allows them to move on.

Remind them that God does have a wonderful plan for their lives that started in the first chapters of Genesis. After humanity rebelled, though, God had to start speaking to us in difficult circumstances, too. We're often confused and surprised by crisis when it happens, and yet this is evidence that God has set eternity in our hearts. (Ecclesiastes 3:11) The fact that we know something like death isn't "right" comes from inherently recognizing it was never God's plan to begin with.

This means that God can draw a straight line to himself using the crooked circumstances that we've ushered into this world. As Christ's representatives, our greatest preparation isn't pop psychology or mimicking advice from daytime talk show personalities. The time you spend with God today is the greatest investment you can make in preparation for effectiveness during any crisis you might be asked to help with tomorrow. The more tied in you are to the Holy Spirit, the better he can guide you with wisdom when the unexpected occurs in your community.

Of course, don't give up spending time with students prior to the next crisis. Relationships are huge before, during, and after it happens. While we can't be there for everyone in every event in the same measure, we can be in quality relationships with others around us that help us truly minister. One youth worker who ministered during the Columbine shootings knows this lesson all too well:

After Columbine, one of the reasons we were so effective was that we were there *before* it happened. In fact, one of the members of our team was actually in the cafeteria when the shootings took place. A bunch of us joined with the parents who were waiting at the elementary school down the street. Then for the next several weeks, about 16 hours a day, we were just with kids. From attending funerals and memorial services with students to simply hanging out with them, we were just with them.

—Heather Snodgrass (former Young Life leader at Columbine High School, 1998 to 2004)[5]

No matter what the crisis is, remember that your mission is to create disciples. You are an agent of God's love, actively, genuinely, and consistently bringing healing by living out Jesus' virtues and attitudes. Your passionate commitment to this mission is indispensable to the young people around you.

So do what you can, and then get the rest you need. The stress level of ministry isn't yours to bear alone, and creating healthy boundaries not only blesses you but also makes room for God to do what God does best…namely, being God. This will also remove the pressure you may put on yourself to see immediate results for your efforts. Remember, Jesus is the Savior, not you.

---

5. Ron Jackson, "Caring Amidst Crisis," *YouthWorker Journal*, March/April 2009.

PART THREE

FOUNDATIONS OF YOUTH MINISTRY III: PROGRAMS AND ENVIRONMENTS

CHAPTER 11

DEVELOPING LEARNERS

I'm going to take a leap of faith and guess that right now you're not wearing a shiny, silver jumpsuit as you read this. (At least, I hope not.) Likewise, there's a good probability that you're not traveling about in a flying car just yet. I'd even venture to say that while we can gain all the nutrition we need from vitamin-like pills, you probably haven't given up the joy of sitting down and enjoying the taste and smells of a good meal.

I mention these things only because for quite some time it's seemed as though these ideas were the benchmarks of our arrival into the "future." From the latest sci-fi movies to old-school cartoons such as *The Jetsons*, humanity's posture has been forward-leaning in anticipation of how things might be different technologically 60 seconds from now. Even Walt Disney World has been required to continually adapt *Tomorrowland* in order to keep it feeling "yesterday-esque."

One benchmark, though, has clearly marked our culture's shift into the future. It initially appeared electronic in nature, but we're seeing it become something more. We once tried to sum it up as the "information age," citing how the Internet has provided us limitless access points to any topic. Others have described our "social networking era," noting how technology has allowed us to connect locally and globally in ways we never could before. Then there is the matter of a "you-centered" world where people can digitally track how you're feeling in the midst of your everyday tasks, or comment on the latest video you've uploaded about a silly thing your dog did.

If you stand back from it all, though, one common thread is more human than industrial—the "absence of the *absence* of knowledge." In other words, no longer do we have to utter the phrase "I don't know" when asked a question, for massive amounts of information are freely available to us when we're willing to execute a few keystrokes. Cell phones have become pocket computers that can access popular search engines just as effectively as laptops. This is more than a change in our machinery—it's also a change in how we live and learn.

Schools are already addressing this issue, forming rules against students using their cell phones during exams. It's ironic: While it seems we're in an era of experimentation, we've also begun to curtail how often we actually think for ourselves. Why learn to spell when the computer will automatically do it for you? What's the point in memorizing geography when you can "Google" the earth?

Our emerging culture has created a potentially dangerous addiction of having immediate and unrestricted access to whatever information we feel we need, whether it's necessary or unnecessary in nature. No longer do we have to live our own lives to gain personal experience, for instead we can "copy and paste" anything we like and pass it off as our own idea. Learning the actual information and memorizing it has become less important than learning how to find the information we need when we need it and say it out loud to sound wiser than we are.

Have you ever stopped to think how this affects the spiritual journeys of your students? Because it does…in more ways than we may realize.

A NECESSARY PARTNERSHIP

In many philosophical circles there's been a debate regarding the importance of knowledge versus wisdom. Perhaps there's value in asking which is more important, but such a question can unconsciously negate their mutually dependent relationship. Knowledge involves accumulating data, and wisdom involves our capacity to apply that data in a proper context. Without either in place, our capacity to grow and learn is stifled.

Consider creation as an example, for God has made it clear through intelligent design that he exists. Many refer to this as "general revelation" in that the whole world creates a message of information we're intended to track back to him. We look at a building and know there was a builder; we look at a painting and know there was a painter; we look at creation and know there is a Creator.

This general revelation has a "specific revelation" as well. The Bible reminds us that "since the creation of the world, God's invisible qualities—his eternal power and divine nature—have been clearly seen, being understood from what has been made, so that people are without excuse" (Romans 1:20). In other words, the knowledge of God acts as a messenger to the Messenger, and God in turn gives us wisdom to live by.

Check out how this approach impacted Moses:

> Now Moses was tending the flock of Jethro his father-in-law, the priest of Midian, and he led the flock to the far side of the desert and came to Horeb, the mountain of God. There the angel of the LORD appeared to him in flames of fire from within a bush. Moses saw that though the bush was on fire it did not burn up. So Moses thought, "I will go over and see this strange sight—why the bush does not burn up."

> When the LORD saw that he had gone over to look, God called to him from within the bush, "Moses! Moses!"

> And Moses said, "Here I am."

> (Exodus 3:1-4)

Note the sequence, including how before his famous spiritual moment Moses first learned what it meant to take care of sheep. No doubt he also accumulated information on ways to survive in the desert, everything from how to find shade on the side of a mountain during the hottest part of the day to noting anything on fire in order to protect the flock from harm. For 40 years Moses spent time as a shepherd, gaining knowledge—and *then* he encountered the burning bush. (Acts 7:30)

Perhaps that's why God used something that was so natural and familiar to Moses in an intriguingly unfamiliar way. On this particular day the mountain he'd learned to rest on no doubt provided shade, giving his mind and body a clearer awareness. As he noted the bush, he was likewise slowed enough to observe that it wasn't burning up the way it was supposed to. What Moses had learned drew him into this new experience, allowing him to connect with God and obtain his wisdom and purpose for life. Ironically, Moses would become a shepherd of people and lead them through desert life for another 40 years.

Have you ever considered why God would do this? Was there a point to the progression of events that occurred that day? Why didn't God just speak to Moses early on in his life without all the theatrics?

THE MYSTERY OF SHARING THE MYSTERY

For many years, the church has taken on the model of dispensing information to whomever would listen. The layout of many gathering spaces speaks volumes about this, from the prominent position of where the teacher stands on a stage or platform to the way the chairs and pews are often positioned around it. This isn't a bad model, but in the emerging culture it's necessary to build bridges to what's already a more interactive generation.

Advertisers have already caught on to this, recognizing that to get you to buy into their products, they can't rely on just selling the truth. Most ads attempt to offer a 30-second experience hoping that once your emotions have engaged in a story, the rest of you will quickly follow. Consider how many commercials in recent years often feature vague images and unclear interactions that seem to only come together in the final few seconds, ultimately revealing the product the narrative has been about the whole time. This approach gets people talking—which perhaps is why even after a big football game like the Super Bowl, you'll find more people in conversation about their favorite commercials than the game itself.

Let's do a hard gut check: Do you sense that the manner in which you're communicating the most amazing truths in the universe is creating a similar interest and buzz among your teens? We're in relationship with the most creative Being ever! The God who came up with the platypus, the human DNA strand, the color green—and yet we often settle for lecture-style "sermons" and fill-in-the-blank handouts for teens. Might there be a better way to develop learners than simply dispensing information? Are there places for mystery, intrigue, and asking questions you can't quickly answer that begin to dignify the size and majesty of our Creator, Savior, Father, and Lord?

Don't get me wrong—our task isn't to mirror the strategic "teasing" the marketplace uses to get you to buy things you don't need. Their hope is to get you to make a purchase, which means that whatever questions asked on the seller's end are self-serving ones. If we ever come across as manipulating students into spiritual decisions so we gain a larger or busier youth ministry, we're no different than corporate America.

Our task is to help students articulate what's going on within them so they better understand the freedom and fully alive life that God offers them. They won't become interested in learning until they realize what they don't know and why they need to know it. Too often we spend time trying to provide answers to questions we haven't given them a reason to ask.

QUESTIONING YOUR QUESTIONS

The position you're in as a youth worker requires you to teach the truths of God and shed light on how to have a personal relationship with him. How you prioritize and define what this means will either turn students into mere receivers of information or help them develop into learners who really "own" their own spiritual journeys. The difference may seem subtle, for our good intentions can blind us to our incomplete actions.

We often see it as our task to give young people the "necessary" facts about God, the plan of salvation, key people in the Bible, and certain verses we believe they should memorize. This may be the job description you were handed, but in and of itself this is deficient and lacking as an on-ramp to lasting growth. I've found that many churches and youth ministries are fond of asking a variation of these four questions:

"Do you know what Jesus did for you?"
"Have you prayed the prayer of salvation yet?"
"Are you in a small group?"
"What ministry are you taking part in?"

Make no mistake, all of these questions should be asked because they deal with establishing an awareness of God, making choices about one's eternal destiny, placing oneself in community, and finding a unique purpose that adds to the kingdom. If they are our only measuring sticks, though, we'll focus on getting a young person to answer them "correctly" so we can move to another individual and ask the very same questions. It's as if our goal isn't to create disciples but to convince others to merely nod their heads at the right times and say the right things. Bagged and tagged.

In a culture exploding with information, maybe our goal shouldn't be to tell young people merely what the truth is, but to help them learn how to identify it for themselves. God is already working in their lives, and behind everything they'll learn or encounter is a redemptive truth of God. Even most ideas and opinions that seem anti-God have teachable aspects to them, from why someone came up with the concept in the first place to where it might lead if taken to an extreme. Consider these other questions we also need to ask to help bring out this awareness:

"As you consider your generation and its views on life, what impact do you suppose it will have on Christianity? What about the other way around—what impact can Christianity have on your generation?"

"What do you believe God's greatest dream is for your life? What's going on inside you when you consider it?"

"If you could travel back to Old Testament times, what would you want to witness? What about this event intrigues you? What might this reveal about your faith?"

"Share with me the questions you have about God. What kinds of questions are your parents asking about God? What can I do to help you start exploring those?"

"Who in your life would you love to see become a Christian? Are you holding back from sharing your faith with him/her in any way? If so, why do you suppose that is?"

"Have you ever considered that the 'normal' things in your life are really miracles, except they happen every day? How does this affect your view of your Creator?"

"What relationships in your life are watering down your connection with Jesus? Name three people who are strengthening your faith."

"What do you believe will be the hardest challenge of your faith in five years? What do you think will be your greatest joy?"

I'm not suggesting abandoning the first set of questions, nor am I saying the second set represents the "new right answers." Certainly, take note of the difference between yes/no questions of agreement versus those that dig into deeper places. Yet, confusing as it sounds, the goal of asking questions isn't to get answers…it's to stimulate young people's capacity to learn so they might become lifetime followers of Jesus Christ.

Where do you think that begins?

Wisdom from the Trenches

One of my Ph.D. professors used to say, "Leaders are learners, and learners are leaders." Perhaps it's a little too cutesy, and it's certainly not accurate 100 percent of the time. Yet I think this wise professor was right. The sharpest leaders I know are the most eager to learn and be transformed; folks who are the most teachable tend to be the most influential.

Students can sense our approach to the learning curve: Do we do the hard work of reading, studying, and dare I say, *thinking*? Or do we assume we can coast on our own charisma or what-worked-so-well-last-year? We don't have to be

Einsteins, and maybe not all of us need more education (although I admit I'm a fan of youth workers seeking more education). What we do need is a contagious curiosity. Then students might just get infected.

—*Kara Powell, 21 years in youth ministry*

A SCARY, BEAUTIFUL THING CALLED "YOUR FAITH"

Can we be honest about something that neither of us wants to be honest about? *You and I don't have all the answers.* No, we aren't omniscient (which means we don't know everything—which, ironically, is why I decided to define *omniscient* just now; don't worry…if you didn't know what it means, I didn't know the first time I heard it, either). There may even be questions deep inside us that we don't like to think about, whether we're afraid of how they may shake our beliefs, or because they simply cannot be addressed in ways we would completely understand.

Imagine if a kid asked you a really good, scary question about God, and you responded with, "You know, I've wondered the same thing." Many times we buy into thinking this is the wrong approach, as if our inability to answer is what pushes kids away from God forever. But you can't put that kind of pressure on yourself because you already know you don't have all the answers.

You do, however, have a relationship with the One who does know the answer—Jesus. In a world full of people and businesses trying to convince teens that they're their new best friends, imagine how refreshing it is when you don't pretend to know more than you do just to win points but instead show kids how questions can be a solid bridge to Christ. Doesn't it sound more authentic when they ask something deep and you respond with, "That's a great question. I'm not sure I can answer that today. Would you mind if I did some reading, and we came back together on it in a few days? Something tells me that God just may be bigger than anything I can come up with on the spot."

Let me be clear—the youth ministry you serve shouldn't be the primary venue for you to figure out your faith. It will certainly bless you in this way, but you need to be a Christ-follower before you're a leader, or else you'll be in the wrong state of mind when theological conversations begin. Take intentional steps to place yourself in discussions with other adults where you can dig up anything you've buried. Taking this approach will help teenagers see you not as an insecure peer but instead as a respectable mentor overflowing with a sense of spiritual wonder.

DEVELOPING LEARNERS

111

The Bible itself tells us to "test" everything and "hold on to what is good" (1 Thessalonians 5:21). This means it's okay to kick the tires of our faith. Much of this happens naturally, and other times it occurs in an unexpected crisis.

Regardless of which process students are engaged in, it's our responsibility—along with the other influencers in their lives—to help them become the best learners they're capable of becoming. In fact, I'd argue that the questions teens are asking about faith are often more revealing than the conclusions they come to. So instead of wondering, *How can I help my students agree with what I'm teaching them?* practice asking yourself, *How can I help my students critically think their way toward conviction?*

"YES, WE'RE OPEN!"

Recall the last time you were about to walk through the door of a local business, only to realize it was closed. In that moment you realized that whatever plans you had in place had to be adjusted, whether that meant returning at a later time or finding another locale to meet your needs in that moment.

I can think of no simpler analogy than this when it comes to what students experience when we close down their authentic faith questions. We have to find a way to hang a metaphorical neon sign around our necks that says, "Yes, we're open!" That also goes for our teaching, our environments, and our conversations—or else our teens will walk away frustrated. (And similar to our two choices at a "closed" sign, they'll either conceal their authentic faith questions and hope for later opportunities to ask them or find someone who will listen and dignify their journeys, even if that person proves a negative influence on their faith.)

Too often we've allowed our healthy desires regarding students forming the "right" thoughts to create unhealthy patterns of *merely telling them what to think*. Remember: Your convictions are your convictions because you've arrived at them on a journey that your students haven't been through. They may take your word on many things, but if your goal is to upload your ideas into them, you'll find it akin to pressing large seeds into very shallow soil. While your ideas may take root for a while and students could very well recite them just as you've taught them to, they'll likely abandon such mantras and slogans when you're no longer active in their lives. In many cases, they'll simply take on the attributes of the newest "loudest voice" in their lives.

Therefore, if you want students to become learners who experience true life change and form lasting convictions about living for God, then you must design your learning (and all other) atmospheres with a spirit of openness. Such environments are:

PERSONAL

You must be involved in students' lives, and they must be involved in yours—and that can be hard and sometimes frustrating. But when you consider the loss of family "community" that many of them are experiencing because of divorce or parents who're always working, this truly is an open door if you're willing to walk into their lives.

MESSY

At times students' choices will be heartbreaking, but it's critical that you help them learn how to "fail forward." One of the greatest sources of inspiration for them to turn negatives into positives is if you're accessible, welcoming, involved, and concerned about the hard things they're going through. You may feel your jaw drop at the things they tell you, but try to see beyond the momentary failures so you can help them envision how God can turn them into good.

CHALLENGING

Loving students in their failures doesn't mean not nudging them in the right directions. Even better, be sure you're telling them God's ideals and teaching them how to think critically before they blow it. Challenging students means you offer answers behind questions, helping them use their thinking processes of choice to arrive at places of conviction. This will be emotional on your end, requiring a lot of prayer, trust, and patience.

FAITH-BASED

If you're teaching and living as a follower of Jesus—and if you're allowing the Holy Spirit to guide you and the direction of your faith community—then be sure your students can observe that you've entrusted their lives (and thinking and convictions) to God as well. They'll know if you haven't.

HUMBLE

We've already established that you don't have all the answers, so introduce students to the sources you rely on. Some of them may be over their heads, but it's comforting for them to know that there are credible voices out there who've come to some great conclusions about matters of faith. In fact, you may even want to show them where different theologians have disagreed on certain beliefs and teach them what it means to practice humility and mutual respect in such matters.

NONJUDGMENTAL

If you're not careful, your youth ministry can become a place where the kids who "sound" like you feel superior to other students who may not. So get rid of unhealthy criticism, disapproval, and negativity that choke the life out of authenticity. Instead foster an open environment, full of grace and encouragement.

FOCUSED ON AUTHENTIC RELATIONSHIPS

Young people long for relationships, desiring a sense of belonging among those of their gender and a sense of approval from the opposite sex. Most of the time they settle for fitting in, for losing pieces of their authentic selves to manufacture "acceptable identities" among their peers. Therefore utilize that common bond of searching for their "selves" within the community to help them realize they don't have to become people they're not in order to discover who God is. Rather their unique differences should be viewed as essential puzzle pieces that "complete the picture" and add to everybody's faith.

LET YOUR PEOPLE GO

When it comes down to it, God uses every experience in our lives to develop our capacity to learn. God's hope is that we learn by living each day on purpose, practicing and patterning our lives on the truths God's passed on to us. God also has always impressed on us that much can be gained if we invest ourselves into a Christ-centered community, as "iron sharpens iron" (Proverbs 27:17). Perhaps in our information-saturated age, this is one way to ensure we haven't slipped on blinders as we access only what our itching ears want to hear. (2 Timothy 4:3)

Take heart, for as complex your ministry to students in this millennium may seem, you'll often find we haven't strayed away from some of the most basic ways people first came to know God. Moses had his burning-bush moment which helped him discover the depths of this God were greater than he imagined:

> Moses said to God, "Suppose I go to the Israelites and say to them, 'The God of your fathers has sent me to you,' and they ask me, 'What is his name?' Then what shall I tell them?"

God said to Moses, "I AM WHO I AM. This is what you are to say to the Israelites: 'I AM has sent me to you.'"

(Exodus 3:13-14)

There were immediate implications for what God shared with Moses, for in the Egyptian culture there was a god for everything. This declaration of identity meant that there was truly only *one* Deity, and that this God was One with…*himself*—the great "I AM." In one sense this was a declaration of truth intended to create knowledge.

However, this pronouncement was intended for more than knowledge. God spoke a Divine truth, stating that his name wasn't "I WAS" or "I WILL BE," but "I AM"—a name rooted in both the present *and* all of eternity. This means that while God is always accessible to us through knowledge—and always will be—there's another component to God that's beyond us. Ultimately our smartest human metaphors will never quite adequately sum up who God is, whether we're trying to figure out the Trinity or understand how a present circumstance has an impact on God's overall plans.

SO LET YOUR PEOPLE GO

This tension hit me during a lunch with an old friend I hadn't seen or spoken to in a decade. As we discussed our faith, I realized that the things coming out of my mouth in that moment were different than the last time we'd talked. I hadn't changed my mind about core things, but I found I had greater wisdom about what *were* the "core things" and what weren't. Over the years of being a Christian, the "I AM" has taken me in for several spiritual overhauls that have helped me realize who God is and who God is not.

And yet I still don't know all of who God is. Each day I find myself asking God to help me forget what I've grown "used to" knowing so that I can re-experience the beauty of learning it all over again—but in a new way or from a different angle. I'd dare say this is something you may want to consider as well, for the things that worked last year in faith and ministry may not be so hot this year.

SO LET YOUR PEOPLE GO!

In a world overflowing with information, the mystery of who God is has again become important. This doesn't mean we ask questions to simply sound profound, but to utilize curiosity to help our teens engage God. When we approach our roles as teachers with this new reality in mind, we may be less inclined to present new information and instead uncover the power of creating environments where we can share and discover powerful truths together.

The goal in developing learners isn't to fill them with facts but to help them encounter the Way, the Truth, and the Life. So commit to the value of your curriculum—but not to the curriculum itself. We're trying to help them be like Jesus, not simply squawk whatever answers we've written in parentheses—assuming that gets the job done. Help students learn *how* they learn, and you just may help them uncover what's most important to learn in the first place...

That God is *their* God, who's gone to great lengths to let them know that they're his people.

CHAPTER 12

DEVELOPING SPIRITUALITY

It's imperative for us to recognize that part of what we've signed up for as volunteer youth workers is guiding teens into forming their own faith. Too often I find that youth ministries lack a model of faith formation to guide teens into developing a faith they not only can own for themselves but also continue to develop on their own.

In the second chapter we looked at a big-picture view of Christian formation. We discovered that it begins with the story of God. And the story of God informs our theology and/or our understanding of God. Our theology, therefore, informs our identities and callings, which answer the questions, "Who am I?" and "What am I called to do?" Out of the development of our identities and callings, we begin to synthesize our experiences and understandings, integrating into our lives certain sets of values or virtues that shape our inner selves. The shaping of our inner lives—or our "way of life"—begins to (and continues to) form the missional behaviors and expressions which we choose to live out for the sake of the world.

Christian formation begins with the convergence of the story of God and one's own story and culminates with working out our faith in a community governed by practices that cooperate with God's mission to restore the world to its intended wholeness. This cannot be done in isolation. It's imperative that youth workers create and sustain a sense and reality of genuine community. It's within the formation of an entire community that individuals are best shaped into growing Christians. This requires that you and I have a robust view of what I refer to as three keys to incorporating teens into congregational community for the purpose of faith formation.

THE THREE KEYS

These three keys are associating, assimilating, and actualizing. *Associating* in its simplest understanding is connecting—it means joining or belonging or being involved. *Assimilating* means integrating or mixing in. *Actualizing* means making it real and lasting.

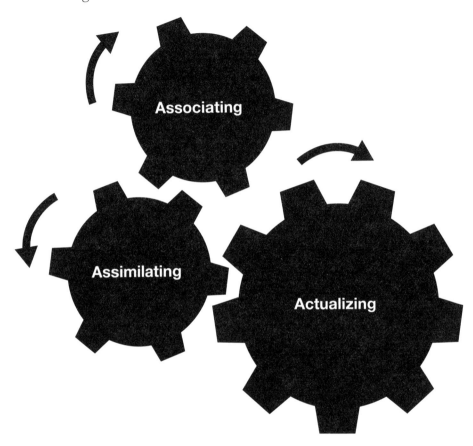

ASSOCIATING

The first phase of faith formation has at least four contingent or dependent dimensions. These dimensions all cooperate with or depend on one another to allow teens to securely belong to communities seeking to guide them toward lives in the way of Jesus. As you think about and evaluate your youth ministry (and the whole of your church), it's in the best interests of your teens if you create a community that:

1. **Consistently offers an invitation to your teens (in the church and community) to participate in the faith.** I've asked many teens in my town why

they aren't connected to a faith community. The reason? *No one asked them!* Teens have an open invitation to participate in our community, but they need that invitation communicated to them regularly.

2. **Consistently welcomes invitees into your community of faith practitioners.** It's one thing to invite teens to participate in your faith community; it's an entirely different thing to make them feel welcome consistently as they explore the community—and long after their initial participation. The invitation is easy; steady, hospitable welcoming can be much harder.

3. **Creates ways in which teens can encounter a loving God or loving people (hopefully both).** Some teens you invite and welcome have decided to connect to your faith community because they're inquiring about God; some are present because they're inquiring about *you*. Either way, they're looking to be loved even before they're looking to belong.

4. **Helps teens find affinity with some of your faith practitioners who ultimately can help them move past an insulated and intermittent development process.** Part of our role as guides is to help teens find affinity with others (i.e., a small group or community in which to learn how to practice their faith). We refer to these smaller groups as *communities of practice*. It's within the context of these communities that teens can learn how to discern the portability and practicability of their faith.

ASSIMILATING

As with associating, the next stage—assimilating—also has four contingent dimensions that help teens' faith formation. (Note: It's important to remember that these dimensions don't work independently of one another but rely on the effective cultivation of the others.) The four dimensions of assimilating are:

1. **Embracing the call toward a budding faith.** Associating demands that teens receive the invitation to participate in community, are welcomed into that community, and can determine what it looks like to live out their faith so they can commit to deeper levels of understanding and practice.

2. **Affirming personal faith by habit, hobby, or holiness.** Some people practice their faith by habit—it just becomes part of their ritualistic lives. Others practice faith as a hobby of sorts, and still others find their true calling is to live a holy life. As this dimension of associating begins to unfold, let habit, hobby, or holiness be the factors of their participation. Teens are working out their faith just like the rest of us—we are all a part of various activities for

various reasons. Don't give up on teens who come as weekly habits or find your youth group to be a hobby—as long as they're participating, they can be called to a life of holiness.

3. **Developing faith through reinforced private and public modeling and shared experience.** The best way for teens to grow in their faith is to see it privately and publically modeled through your participation. Don't ever think that teens in your group aren't watching you…*they watch nearly every move you make.* Your reliability, relationships, commitment—they watch you! And they learn how to practice their faith by watching you practice yours.

4. **Calculating pockets of isolation from private and public reinforcement in order to question, doubt, resist, resent, etc.** Through modeling the practice of faith, teens begin to experience it through their own experiences, not yours. Although you share your life with them as you model the faith, it's through the convergence of their own experiences that they develop a "take" or a position on their future experiences with faith.

ACTUALIZING

After teens have been in association with a community of practice and have assimilated into the personal expression of a communal experience, they begin the process of actualizing their faith.

This means making it real—completely their own—but not in isolation or for the sake of a pious individualism. Rather, an ongoing actualization of faith is for the sake of the community of practice and for the sake of the world. I say this often when I teach workshops—I'm not interested in creating a bunch of spiritual narcissists or teens on their way toward becoming adults who have individualistic perspectives of faith.

Actualizing the faith involves the following:

1. **Embodying the faith through cause, conviction, and motivation.** When teens begin to make their faith real by actualizing it, they develop a set of reasons—causes, convictions, and motivations—to continue in the practice of their faith. You'll know teens are growing in the faith when they move past the associating elements of habit and hobby and move toward lives driven by holiness or complete love for God and others.

2. **Accepting the idea that process doesn't always mean progress.** I'm a big believer in the *process* of faith practice. As I've already mentioned in this book (and on the accompanying videos), we don't make finished products—

we guide unfinished people through a process of faith discovery. However (and it's a big "however"), process doesn't always mean progress. When teens actualize their faith through our guidance, they realize the importance of progress—or moving forward in their faith development.

3. **Developing a rule of life that shapes the way a faith-full life is privately and publicly articulated.** Part of the progress is the development of a rule of life (or a set of virtues) that shapes the way teens express their faith and apply it to everyday life. You know teens are growing in their faith when their articulation of it resembles what their peers are being led by.

4. **Commitment to an enduring path of progress marked by increased frequency and duration of the holy moments in one's life.** When teens' faith is actualized, they experience holiness more often and for longer periods of time. This isn't true only for teens; it's true for adults, too. An actualized faith also provides opportunities for us to live holy lives marked by an increase in the duration of the holy or sacred experiences and moments in life.

MAKING IT WORK

Teens' faith formation is what we signed up for—but it certainly isn't solely on us. We must find ways to engage the other adults in our teens' lives to help provide robust opportunities to develop a faith formed from within a community of practice—one that sees the importance of a holistic formation journey.

Many times I find—in my interactions with youth ministries of all sizes—that the faith-formation process is the last thing youth workers think about. We're so consumed by the seemingly thousands of things bombarding us 24/7 that we tend toward mere completion of tasks (scheduling events, attending activities, organizing trips, recruiting volunteers, etc.) and neglect (and sometimes abandon) the key to helping teenagers on their way toward a lasting and fruitful and always-forming faith.

The next time you ask yourself, "Why did I sign up for this?" or you question your purpose (you are not alone, by the way), please remember that your purpose is to guide students into Christian formation for the mission of God by creating a community that helps teens associate, assimilate, and actualize their faith.

CHAPTER 13

DEVELOPING MISSION

I'm a big sucker for inspirational speeches in movies. It's as if the screenwriters put their best efforts into those brief monologues so that everyone listening onscreen (as well as in the theater) is stirred up to accomplish something. It may be "the big game" some team needs to win, a battle where the odds are stacked against the good guys, or a way of life that's worth fighting for, with every ounce of our energy.

You have come to fight as free men, and free men you are. What will you do with that freedom? Will you fight?...Aye, fight and you may die, run and you'll live. At least a while. And dying in your beds many years from now, would you be willing to trade all the days from this day to that for one chance, just one chance, to come back here and tell our enemies that they may take our lives, but they'll never take our freedom!

—*William Wallace (Mel Gibson)*, Braveheart

You're five feet nothin', a hundred and nothin', and you've got hardly a speck of athletic ability. And you hung in with the best college football team in the land for two years. And you're also gonna walk outta here with a degree from the University of Notre Dame. In this lifetime you don't have to prove nothin' to nobody except yourself. And after what you've gone through, if you haven't done that by now—it ain't gonna never happen. Now go on back...

—*Fortune (Charles S. Dutton)*, Rudy

Hold your ground, hold your ground! Sons of Gondor, of Rohan, my brothers! I see in your eyes the same fear that would take the heart of me. A day may come when the courage of men fails, when we forsake our friends and break all bonds of fellowship, but it is not this day. An hour of woes and shattered shields, when the age of men comes crashing down! But it is not this day! This day we fight!

—*Aragorn (Viggo Mortensen)*, The Lord of the Rings: The Return of the King

They're not that different from you, are they? Same haircuts. Full of hormones, just like you. Invincible, just like you feel. The world is their oyster. They believe they're destined for great things, just like many of you; their eyes are full of hope, just like you. Did they wait until it was too late to make from their lives even one iota of what they were capable? Because, you see gentlemen, these boys are now fertilizing daffodils. But if you listen real close, you can hear them whisper their legacy to you. Go on, lean in. Listen. You hear it?...'Carpe...' Hear it?... 'Carpe...carpe diem. Seize the day, boys; make your lives extraordinary.'

—*John Keating (Robin Williams),* Dead Poets Society

These stirring moments in film seem to leap off the screen and into our hearts, causing ordinary dialogue in fictional art to become a well-needed jab forward in our very real lives. Maybe this is due largely in part to the need we all have for someone to challenge us beyond status-quo lives. When we see it on the silver screen, we find ourselves tempted to jump into the movie, pick up a sword, and join in the good fight.

Have you ever considered that your life and voice have the same power? Or that the students you lead are yearning for someone to call that "best effort" out of them? What about the community and world full of students who will benefit from your ministry having a clear picture of what could be and should be?

Maybe you don't envision yourself in a movie moment with a powerful orchestra underscoring everything you say. Nonetheless, there is tremendous power in you to point at a goal, and in your own words declare, "That's the next hill we need to take...we *must* take...or else all is lost." Whether you have the luxury of a stage and a microphone, or you're sitting across a restaurant table with a couple of students who've given you their attention, you're meant to challenge the people around you forward toward their greatest-possible lives.

So the first question you need to ask: *What am I going to challenge them toward?*

Wisdom from the Trenches

I think that a lot of volunteers in youth ministry defer to the paid youth staff to develop a mission. But volunteers, too, can get serious about having a specific mission. The question is—what do you, in particular, have to offer teenagers?

It might be a hobby—like working on old cars; or it might be a gifting—like prayer. You might decide that you're better with middle schoolers than high schoolers, or that you prefer leading a small group to being a camp counselor. All of these factors should be prayerfully considered as you, yourself, determine your mission as a volunteer youth worker.

—Tony Jones, 18 years in youth ministry

A MISSION AFFECTS EVERYTHING

Think about one of the greatest events, lessons, or activities you've ever done (or seen done) in youth ministry. Do you have the sense that it was just a really good idea at the time or that it propelled the ministry forward? Both outcomes have their place, but the difference between good ideas and exceedingly great ideas is that the former have a function for the moment while the latter point to the big idea of your youth ministry.

You'll see this as you consider and learn from some of the many great youth ministry models. They're held up in the spotlight for a reason. But don't forget—the reason isn't so we can use their terminology and concepts without question. Many leaders opt for copy-driven concepts that look good on paper but are actually shadowy versions of what God intended their unique ministries to authentically be. What *really* works in one ministry context *can* work in another, but preventing God from birthing a burden in your heart means you'll always be photocopying someone else's passion.

Have you ever had the sense that while you were putting something on your calendar you weren't quite sure why you were doing it? I don't mean to imply that you weren't putting it there on purpose, but did you really understand what that activity's core purpose was? More specifically, as you penciled in that event, did you have an unmistakable, crystal-clear understanding of the greatest thing that could possibly happen in the life of another through whatever you'd scribbled down?

The thing you need to wrestle with is what the big idea of your youth ministry is.

Knowing this allows you to identify whether your calendar is a to-do list or a must-do list. This is a highly contagious matter, too, for it will mark the difference in whether your students simply do things that have been *labeled* with Christ or are taking part in things that make them *like* Christ.

A truly contagious mission can happen on all levels of your ministry, but it requires this flow:

Your LORD must build it.
Your HEART must overflow it.

Your PASTOR must champion it.

Your STUDENTS must own it.

Your ADULTS must coach it.

Your ELDERS must understand it.

YOUR LORD MUST BUILD IT: DEFINING THE DIFFERENCE

The King James Bible states, in Proverbs 29:18, that "Where there is no vision, the people perish." Contrast this thought with how in recent years there has been much written on the topic of vision through the eyes of the business world.

Indeed we've gained much through such corporate insights, but we've also regrettably begun understanding this verse solely through a business lens. We read about the need for "vision" and assume we're supposed to break out some dry erase markers and a whiteboard to write down our own ideas of what should happen. Such brainstorming can play a healthy role later in the process of developing a mission, but it isn't where we're intended to begin.

More contemporary translations of the Bible have recognized this unfortunate misinterpretation of culture, taking us back to the true nature of the original language. For instance, the New International Version reads, "Where there is no revelation, people cast off restraint." This is an important clarity, for while a revelation is always a vision, a vision is not always a revelation.

Developing a mission for youth work is all about recognizing that difference. A God-built ministry by definition means that *God must build it*. You'll be required to put in the sweat of seeking and waiting upon God, discerning through Scripture and the Holy Spirit's leading what God ultimately wants to do. On both the macro level of your entire ministry's mission and the micro level of what God wants to accomplish in the lives of individual students, it's up to you to be sure that it's *not* up to you.

In both situations, a God-built vision will always sync up with what God's doing in the ultimate version of his Story. It may sound strange to consider this, but what you do in the small slice of the world you live in is a powerful piece of a mosaic that includes the great epic events of the Scriptures. You're surrounded by a cloud of witnesses who cheer you on, which means that there is always a larger, more encompassing context for everything you do. (Hebrews 12:1) So when there's that internal nudge to invest your energy into a person or event, know that there's more weight to your response than a simple yes or no.

But when this takes place, the upside is that you can have great confidence that what you're doing is making a lasting and eternal impact. The local church exists for such a burden, for rather than merely being frustrated with the way things are in our world and the spiritual condition of humanity, we're called by God to let our lives become conduits for God to change everything from the inside out. And over time you'll see that by joining God, you're doing more than fulfilling a job description as a youth worker; in fact, you're offering a heart of obedience that grows your relationship with him.

And as this heart grows, it becomes able to carry more significant burdens.

YOUR HEART MUST OVERFLOW IT: A CUPBEARER'S BURDEN

After Israel's first three human kings died, there were several disputes regarding who would take over and how God's people would be governed. The once-strong kingdom split into a northern and southern political structure, during which the Lord sent several prophets to warn the Jews that this would ultimately lead to their enemies overtaking them. And this is exactly what happened, as the children of Israel were scattered into captivity under foreign rulers.

But one of these powerful kings (from Persia) decided to begin releasing the Jews back to their land. The book of Ezra records how the Jews' first priority upon returning home was to begin worshiping God through the restoration of a daily altar and the rebuilding of the temple. Meanwhile, the once strong walls of Jerusalem remained devastated, providing no defense against potential attacks or insults from surrounding peoples. Those proclaimed to share the light of the world had become an international joke.

Back in Persia, a Jewish man named Nehemiah was enjoying the good life of being the king's cupbearer. This job allowed him to eat choice food and drink—but it wasn't a form of hospitality. Nehemiah protected the king against poisoning by chewing the first bite and taking the first sip. This is the context at play at the beginning of his book:

> The words of Nehemiah son of Hakaliah: In the month of Kislev in the twentieth year, while I was in the citadel of Susa, Hanani, one of my brothers, came from Judah with some other men, and I questioned them about the Jewish remnant that survived the exile, and

also about Jerusalem. They said to me, "Those who survived the exile and are back in the province are in great trouble and disgrace. The wall of Jerusalem is broken down, and its gates have been burned with fire."

When I heard these things, I sat down and wept. For some days I mourned and fasted and prayed before the God of heaven. Then I said: "LORD, the God of heaven, the great and awesome God, who keeps his covenant of love with those who love him and keep his commandments, let your ear be attentive and your eyes open to hear the prayer your servant is praying before you day and night for your servants, the people of Israel…"

(Nehemiah 1:1-6)

This prayer continues on to the end of the chapter, but notice how it begins: When Nehemiah heard about something happening to his people more than 800 miles away, he allowed himself to feel the full weight of their burden. Instead of enjoying the perks of his privileged lifestyle and the freedom to "not care," he physically sat down and began to weep. Soon prayer flowed out of him as he shared with God everything from an acknowledgment of his own sin to that of his people. He ends with a hope that the Lord will open up the doors for him to do something about it through his relationship with the king.

When was the last time you let your heart break in this way? When you set aside your life's comforts in order to feel the pain of another? It's natural to keep a protective guard up; there seem to be too many burdens in the world for our emotions to keep up with. Unfortunately, some of us get so used to protecting our hearts that we never let them fully react and respond to what God is weeping over. And protecting ourselves only takes us down solitary and deceptive paths where life seems safer than it actually is.

In this vein, I dare you to receive what may sound like a complicated challenge. In the next few days, go to a place where teenagers hang out—a local school, mall, park, church, or recreation center. Sit down where you can see most of the teens and ask God to develop in you a deep love for each of them. It may seem overwhelming to attempt this, for whether you know them or not you're running the risk of caring more than you do right now. Once you ask God to open the eyes of your heart, though, God will start a process in you that will make you more than a youth worker…it will make you a youth *lover*. And that's just the kind of person he can use to change a generation.

YOUR PASTOR MUST CHAMPION IT: SHOWING RESPECT

It's obvious Nehemiah became a man full of passion regarding what God had broken him over. Such zeal, though, can be both illuminating and blinding if we forget our context. Nehemiah didn't, opting instead to take a posture of fearful respect for the leader he served. Notice the pattern by which he shares it with his employer, the king of Persia:

> In the month of Nisan in the twentieth year of King Artaxerxes, when wine was brought for him, I took the wine and gave it to the king. I had not been sad in his presence before; so the king asked me, "Why does your face look so sad when you are not ill? This can be nothing but sadness of heart."
>
> I was very much afraid, but I said to the king, "May the king live forever! Why should my face not look sad when the city where my ancestors are buried lies in ruins, and its gates have been destroyed by fire?"
>
> The king said to me, "What is it you want?"
>
> Then I prayed to the God of heaven, and I answered the king, "If it pleases the king and if your servant has found favor in his sight, let him send me to the city in Judah where my ancestors are buried so that I can rebuild it."
>
> Then the king, with the queen sitting beside him, asked me, "How long will your journey take, and when will you get back?" It pleased the king to send me; so I set a time.
>
> (Nehemiah 2:1-6)

There is no question that Nehemiah was ready to articulate his mission out loud with intensity. Yet the first thing out of his mouth is, "May the king live forever," followed later by, "If it pleases the king and if your servant has found favor in his sight." Here Nehemiah models a unique self-control and respect that we can all learn something from. While Nehemiah's burden was God-given, he didn't let the righteous component become a *self-righteous* stumbling block in his interaction with the king. Far too often those with holy burdens assume they don't have to recognize the human authority over them, creating a host of issues that can otherwise be avoided.

I wish I could say that I've learned this lesson about diplomacy through great foresight, but it's one I've developed due to regrettable hindsight. Over the years I've at times found myself thinking I was a part of the most important ministry in the church and that my efforts demanded the best resources (even if it meant other ministries suffered). To top it off, the way I shared this made any "right" passion in me come across all wrong. Maybe you know this struggle of trying to share what

God's put inside you so that others feel inspired to join in. It takes more time and isn't easy, but it does help people feel valued instead of spoken down to.

Ironically, I've been on the other end, too. Once when I was scheduled to be away from our weekly ministry gathering, I invited a special speaker to come in. When I gave him some general guidelines regarding the length of time he would have to speak, he pushed back and told me that he was going to do whatever God wanted him to do, whether it went over the allotted time or not. I recognized and respected a measure of righteous conviction in what he said but felt he was blindly presuming that God wasn't speaking through me as someone empowered by God to serve over that ministry. Wanting to reconcile the matter, I decided to move some things around for him so he'd have extra time to teach, and he assured me that he would honor my request of when to end the service.

In the end, though, this speaker still went 30 minutes longer than our normal service. He felt justified in his actions, primarily because someone came to Jesus through an elongated altar call he gave. I certainly celebrated that when I returned, but I was also troubled to learn that a meeting we'd planned that day to deal with an important church matter had to be canceled because of this time issue. This created several other problems, leading to several families pulling out of our church.

Reflecting on it all, of course I'd always choose someone coming to Jesus that day versus angering a few people who are already believers. Yet I wonder if this speaker could've come in with a different spirit that made his ministry feel more like a partnership versus a solo project. After listening to the recording of the message given that day, I'd also argue that much of it could have been trimmed, and there still would have been an appropriate opportunity to invite that person who responded (if not more) to make a decision for Jesus. Maybe what we think of as the "authority against us" is sometimes more accurately "us against the authority."

There is something to be said about this in your capacity as a volunteer youth worker. You may be justified in your feeling that you aren't getting the space, budget, resources, or attention that you, your ministry, and your students deserve; on the other hand, though, you may be missing something that substantiates why the church is offering you the framework that it is. Either way, it's up to *you* to submit yourself to the authority over you, for they have been established by God. (Romans 13:1-7)

"Have confidence in your leaders and submit to their authority," Hebrews 13:17 challenges. "Because they keep watch over you as those who must give an account.

Do this so that their work will be a joy, not a burden, for that would be of no benefit to you."

Take these words to heart, and the potential payoff is gaining a pastor/leader over you who's a champion of what God has placed in your heart to disciple a generation back to God. A lot of churches are filled with pastors who know that "something" needs to happen for teenagers, so they hand off the baton to you, hoping that you'll manage it. Imagine the difference, though, of helping them "get it" as you respectfully share the burden on your heart and show them how it fits into the greater plans of God's kingdom.

Maybe this is why the king asked Nehemiah, "What is it that you want?" If you don't realize it, this would be like receiving a blank check from your local public school officials to fund your youth group. We're told that part of this is due to Nehemiah having found favor in the king's sight, but I also believe Nehemiah's promise to return played into things, too. Senior leaders like it when they can see how your actions on a specific level play into what they're attempting on a church-wide scale. This is why a foreign king was comfortable supporting the rebuilding of a land he would not control, and why he sent off Nehemiah with money, support, and resources from the royal treasury.

Picture a version of that in your church where those in your congregation with the greatest influence speak favorably and supportively of the mission stirring within you. Maybe it's time you meet with them, not just to share your mission but to also gain a clearer understanding of their mission. If you're going to better explain how the student ministry fits within the overall purpose and vision of the church, you need to first understand them.

YOUR STUDENTS MUST OWN IT: INSPECTING THE WALLS

With all the resources he needed at his disposal and the credibility to lead, Nehemiah again paused before taking action. Upon arriving in the city, he took some time at night to inspect the ruins of the old walls.

> By night I went out through the Valley Gate toward the Jackal Well and the Dung Gate, examining the walls of Jerusalem, which had been broken down, and its gates, which had been destroyed by fire...The officials did not know where I had gone or what I was doing, because as yet I had said nothing to the Jews or the priests or nobles or officials or any others who would be doing the work. Then I said to them, "You see the trouble we are in:

Jerusalem lies in ruins, and its gates have been burned with fire. Come, let us rebuild the wall of Jerusalem, and we will no longer be in disgrace." I also told them about the gracious hand of my God on me and what the king had said to me.

They replied, "Let us start rebuilding." So they began this good work.

(Nehemiah 2:13, 16-18)

This insight provided Nehemiah with context, ensuring that whatever goals he set were true to reality and not based on perception alone. It also afforded him a sense of confidence when criticism kicked in. After all, it's easier to generate enthusiasm when you believe in something yourself.

The analogy is obvious, isn't it? Everything you can read in this book and any other resource will never replace studying what's actually happening in the lives of the young people you serve. You can set goals in a vacuum or do things because someone told you that you should. To actually see them accomplished, though, you must be sure that they make sense to the students themselves. When that happens, the appropriate buy-in can take place.

Nehemiah is well aware of this, which is why he encourages a pattern of ownership you may see in these verses:

Adjoining this, Jedaiah son of Harumaph made repairs opposite his house.

(3:10)

Next to him, Baruch son of Zabbai zealously repaired another section, from the angle to the entrance of the house of Eliashib the high priest.

(3:20)

Beyond them, Benjamin and Hasshub made repairs in front of their house; and next to them, Azariah son of Maaseiah, the son of Ananiah, made repairs beside his house.

(3:23)

Above the Horse Gate, the priests made repairs, each in front of his own house. Next to them, Zadok son of Immer made repairs opposite his house.

(3:28-29)

If you were rebuilding the wall near your house, you'd make every effort to be sure it was incredibly strong—and you certainly don't want the weakest point in the wall to be near your family when the enemies attack. So it only made sense for each person to take ownership of the vision in a way that personally affected him.

The Bible describes this passion as people working "zealously" to accomplish the mission. (Nehemiah 3:20) In fact, it soon became contagious as neighbors started blessing neighbors, and within a short amount of time much was accomplished.

Think about what it might look like to allow your students to have this kind of ownership in the youth ministry—a balance of an overarching mission combined with hands-on ownership. In many youth groups, though, we tend to see one of two extremes:

1. **The adult youth worker plans it all:** If you're the only one entering events and activities on your calendar, you're missing out on injecting some passion and perspective into your students that would send waves of enthusiasm inside and outside your ministry. Even a student who doesn't yet believe in Jesus can take ownership of setting up chairs or planning games, not to mention your kids who "get it" and who are willing to coordinate your prayer time. So the next time you sit down to plan out your next season of ministry, be sure that you're not alone.

2. **The young people plan it all:** This approach sounds like a great idea in theory, but without adult guidance and an overarching mission, it will probably backfire. Young people should be given the chance to design events, outreaches, and studies. However, they shouldn't be left to do so without healthy boundaries, or else the most influential personalities in the group will take over. Every student has "nice" ideas about what to do, but that doesn't make these ideas the "best" ideas. If left unchecked, one person's passion can become such a distraction to the whole group that no one feels empowered to push back.

Nehemiah struck the right balance, for before he deployed people into any form of work he first inspected the walls himself. In your context, think of how this translates as you let the flow of what God is forming in you create a framework for discussions. Instead of sitting down with teens and asking, "So, what do you want to do?" you would be saying, "This is what I see in the Bible and what God has been burning into me about what needs to happen in and through our ministry. Can I take you on a similar study and journey with God so that we can figure out what he is stirring inside of you?"

Sitting down with students and helping them dream is akin to playing metaphorical pinball. We need to empower teens to roam free all over the board with God, but it's our task to serve as the flippers, ensuring they avoid the gutters and stay in the game to score all the points God says they can. Practically, this involves you beginning the "launch" well by entering into dialogue with students about what God said could and should happen when all is said and done. As things play on, you continue to serve by helping them bounce out of traps and into better places and by talking with them about what needs to happen in them and to them.

If you can impart this value well, you will have shown youth what it means to live in submission under God, his church, and a healthy leader. This is a skill they can take with them for life, for the Bible tells us that the "greatest thing" that Jesus Christ wants to see accomplished in your midst will always take place in community.

YOUR ADULTS MUST COACH IT: GUARDING THE GOOD WORK

As the wall building continued, the taunts and threats from surrounding communities escalated. Nehemiah responded with a team approach:

> Therefore I stationed some of the people behind the lowest points of the wall at the exposed places, posting them by families, with their swords, spears and bows. After I looked things over, I stood up and said to the nobles, the officials and the rest of the people, "Don't be afraid of them. Remember the Lord, who is great and awesome, and fight for your families, your sons and your daughters, your wives and your homes."
>
> From that day on, half of my men did the work, while the other half were equipped with spears, shields, bows and armor. The officers posted themselves behind all the people of Judah who were building the wall. Those who carried materials did their work with one hand and held a weapon in the other, and each of the builders wore his sword at his side as he worked. But the man who sounded the trumpet stayed with me.
>
> (Nehemiah 4:13-14; 16-18)

Do you have someone like this in your life who helps guard the good work of your mission? Sometimes it's another with whom we share equal responsibility in youth ministry; other times it's a team of volunteers who step in to support you in both regular and irregular ways. No matter how it plays out, we have to have other adults engaged with us as we serve students and pursue the unique calling God has put forth for us all.

Early on in ministry, my approach to this was to have one volunteer who was directly responsible for about six students in our ministry. The more I've seen this play out, though, the more I wonder if that ratio needs to be reversed. It almost seems like we need a team of people investing into every student from every angle possible. Maybe it shouldn't be up to one person to play basketball, teach a lesson, send birthday cards, cook hamburgers, pop in on them at work, and so forth when there are plenty of people in your church who could do a piece of that.

In saying that, I don't mean to negate all of the challenges you've already read about thus far in this book. It is a good idea to visit kids at school when you can, sit down with them and tinker on the guitar, or have a movie night at your house so you can connect. You already know, though, that you can't do this all on your own and will grow tired if you try. So why would you even try to do it that way?

Perhaps because it's more convenient to just take on the load by yourself than to find others willing to join you. Maybe when we think of a word such as *recruitment,* we sigh at the energy it may take to effectively bring in new people and get them trained. If this is your focus, it's all wrong; if you feel this way, you need to start thinking differently. What if, instead of asking people to "help you" with your load, you pulled a Huckleberry Finn approach and spoke with them about the opportunity they'd "get to" be a part of. Be cautious, though: Attempting to get people to join you by begging often creates a team full of people who're there because they'd feel guilty if they weren't.

Remember what we've covered with student ownership, too. In all of this you aren't merely trying to get people to follow you and help you lead, but also you have a unique opportunity to help *them* lead. Everyone has a different take on how we should spend our time on this throughout the week, but I'd argue that if you aren't spending at least a third of your time investing into other adult leaders, you'll burn out fast. But if you increase that amount, you'll find yourself doing more than surviving—you'll actually be thriving in this area.

We need people who will fight for us when we're attacked, trade places when we're tired, and sound off encouragement that rallies us back to what matters most. Many times they possess skill sets we lack—bringing everything from music, mechanics, and the arts to sports—with levels of competency that bless students and your overall ministry. All this helps guard the good work of the mission and offers you the motivation that we're all in this together.

YOUR ELDERS MUST UNDERSTAND IT: SPREADING GOOD GOSSIP

Every church has a set of people who guard the perceived big picture of that congregation. Often it's formalized, and they are literally called "elders" or the "church board." In newer churches this may be the launch team that helps the lead pastor get things off the ground; in unhealthy situations, it may be people who've donated the most financially and assume they've earned positions of influence because of it. Sometimes these individuals simply represent close friendships the pastoral staff has with others (which often creates the conversation at meetings or in sermons that begins with, "I've heard from a few people that…").

Whomever these people are and whatever level of health your congregation has, the bottom line is that they hold influence over others. It may be that these influencers possess a large sway over those who listen to them whenever they speak—or they may be well positioned on the local grapevine and spread information quickly. They can do all of this during meetings within the four walls of the building, as well as informally by hanging out at someone's house and sharing opinions about the church and its leaders.

There's a good chance you've noted positive and negative impacts these people have left upon the church, but you may not have realized that you can affect *them* with the mission God has given you before they affect you. We often overlook or resent such people and the influence they hold (perhaps because we don't have that kind of power?), seldom bringing them into the purity of our passion. There will be times when you can turn them into friends and allies, and other times that you simply have to hold your ground while they chip away because of misunderstanding.

Nehemiah encountered both. In one instance, the people were crying out how their own countrymen with privileges were holding them in a form of bondage since food was so scarce. Nehemiah spoke with these people in power and helped them see how they were slowing down the work of God without realizing it. The Bible records that initially "they kept quiet, because they could find nothing to say," and then later they came on board and stated they wouldn't demand anything more from them. (Nehemiah 5:8, 12)

Later Nehemiah encountered people scheming to harm him, saying they wanted to meet with him. Nehemiah replied by sending messengers who said: "I am carrying on a great project and cannot go down. Why should the work stop while I leave it and go down to you?" (Nehemiah 6:1-4). This happened four times, and four times he gave them the same answer. The fifth time they even made up a story that "some of the people" were going to revolt from within, and Nehemiah countered back, "Nothing like what you are saying is happening; you are just making it up out of your head" (Nehemiah 6:8).

These Scriptures show us that there are few things these influential people will need to receive from you before their position of influence can truly work *for* you instead of against you:

YOUR RESPECT

Whether they've earned your relational respect or not, these people are in authority and deserve your respect on at least one level—prayer. The more you lift them up before God, the better you'll understand the worth God says they possess. Likewise you'll find yourself less intimidated by their human authority when you place them next to the authority of God. The upside is that if they're using their influence wisely, you'll also begin to see how it fits into God's ultimate plan.

YOUR HONESTY

Take the initiative to share your dreams and not speak in generalities when specific words can have a stronger impact. Even if they disagree, you gain respect when you speak truth. If there's ever a question about what you value, the people you've shared your heart with will be able to speak clearly to answer that uncertainty.

YOUR EDUCATION

You're becoming a better youth culture expert every day, but most everyone else in your church isn't on that learning curve. When you add a line item to your budget for a video game system or a shipment of a certain book you'll study with the students, they may need an explanation about why these things are on your list. It may feel like they're against you, but the reality is that they don't know what you've come to understand. (And who do you think is supposed to help them understand?)

LEARNING THE HARD WAY

I've learned the hard way that all of these things matter—because the relationships you have (or don't have) with such people affect more individuals and plans than you realize.

Once I planned a huge youth event that involved bringing in a special speaker, musicians, and all the logistics of promotion and management. I'd received approval for the event from my senior pastor four months ahead of time, and our church board was informed right after his approval. Part of the event was financially covered by other churches that got involved, and we had planned to pick up the remainder through a donation that a friend of mine made to the youth group. This meant (at least in my mind) that nothing would have to be spent from the church budget... until the questions began.

Soon three members of the church board informally met with the pastor the night before the event and told him they weren't comfortable with my spending anything more than $50 out of the church budget on this event. (*So what,* right? *We were covered…* Well, not exactly.) I viewed the gift my friend gave as not part of the budget—but some church board members decided later that they didn't view it that way. So with everyone flying in the next day, the promotion we'd invested in around town, and the arrangements we'd made with the school, this news initially worried me.

I'll be honest: I still don't know if I was "offsides" in this line of thinking because of the awkward 11th-hour position that I felt I was put in. I'd covered my bases months ahead and gotten approval from within our church to sign contracts and make financial commitments. We'd prayed for the event, coordinated student ownership in how things were promoted, knew God was in it, and even brought in the extra money from the outside to cover our expenses.

The success of the event was beyond anyone's expectations. We helped 40 students come to Christ that night, not to mention the countless others who made recommitments to God and took steps forward to start prayer groups on their campuses. Everything went well logistically, and all the volunteer youth workers felt it was a powerful event that inspired them to keep pouring into students. We even witnessed a new bond beginning to form among the young people who, while they attended different churches, started connecting more as "one church" on their campuses.

And yet the questions continued.

At the next board meeting I was asked to attend, I began to feel the frustration of the people who tried to persuade me in a different direction. They didn't see the donated money as I did and took it as disrespect that I chose to honor our commitment to do the event. I still remember the senior pastor trying to sum things up by asking, "So, what have we learned from this?" and one man responding, "We've learned that the voice of the board doesn't mean anything."

All of this underscores the reality we face in ministry when people of influence don't understand what we're doing and why we're doing it in the first place. Again, these are people you may or may not officially answer to, but in many ways they add to the climate of what you're doing. When you ask for approval for an activity or funds, you'll make better headway if you've had a "meeting before the meeting."[6] Put in some quality time regarding what you present to them (as well as how you present it), and you just may find positive gossip spreading about the youth ministry

---

6. This phrase has been best attributed to John Maxwell.

and its leadership. Otherwise you may find the questions about your ministry will lead to a climate in which people question *you*.

"ANOTHER BRICK IN THE WALL"

As you consider the mission before you, you'll have moments of tremendous success in achieving it. You'll also experience resistance, setbacks, and even what may feel like permanent destruction. When God is involved, though, the story never ends with a period.

The whole account of Nehemiah is in the Bible because the once-great walls originally in place were destroyed and needed to be rebuilt. Nehemiah and his people did reach their goal, and the new walls stood tall for hundreds of years. Then in 70 AD another country in power tore down the walls again. End of the story, right?

According to the bigger picture of eternity, not quite. While this destruction of Jerusalem was tragic, it was also symbolic in that it occurred after Jesus had walked the earth, was killed, and was then resurrected. Christ reestablished the possibility for the whole world to reconcile with God, and the early church began to overflow this proclamation first in Jerusalem, and then Judea and Samaria, and then to the uttermost parts of the world. By the time the walls were destroyed, it was as if God was saying, "No longer is there one place where my people live. This destruction actually shows the great promise of construction."

I hope that as we've read through these Scriptures you've allowed them to read you. Success and failure are a part of life, but the good news with God is that even when it ends poorly, God is able to bring a redemptive slant to things. Don't judge your value by the size of your youth group or in how many students like you. Remember what the big idea is, what God has told you your ministry is about, and then make your decisions in accordance with it.

Your confidence won't come from others but from your relationship with Jesus Christ. Stay confident as you follow him, for at times he may dare you to do things that run against the grain of what everyone else believes is the right way to go. He will, though, also empower you when everything seems backward in your students and the overall youth culture. Everyone will be looking for someone to point them forward to Jesus, so clear your throat, step up to the microphone, and believe that whatever God has put into your heart will come out of your mouth and make a difference in achieving a mission bigger than any of us.

It always does, even if you feel you've accomplished nothing.

Everything you do in the name of Jesus is another brick in the wall.

CHAPTER 14

DEVELOPING COMMUNITY

Without a doubt, *community* has become a buzzword in recent years as we've attempted to better address our lack of connection (though the Bible tells us it's been happening since people first experienced a desire to hide their nakedness—Genesis 3:7).

It's not uncommon for teenagers to find some area of their lives in which there's detachment from others with whom they'd like to be in better relationships. For many it may be those at school or work who give them a lifeless handshake, a cold shoulder, or rolling eyeballs. Others find it in their extracurricular activities, as the team concept never truly translates since their peers in power create unwritten rules for acceptance.

Let's examine some unique trends worth tracking in this particular youth culture.

The baby boomers were the first Americans to significantly accelerate divorce statistics to the level we find them today. Households were affected in that moment and into the future as kids saw firsthand what happens when parents redefine marriage from meaning "commitment" to meaning "convenience." As adults attempted to pacify relational deficits in whatever way they could, it wasn't uncommon to find several vacations and extravagant gifts paid for by credit cards they couldn't ultimately afford to pay. Many in the generation that followed vowed that when they formed families of their own, it was going to be "different."

This next baton pass is what we're in the midst of right now, as those kids have grown up to become the parents of the kids you now serve. You may see some of the fruit of this generational reaction looking to not repeat the mistakes of their pre-decessors—in both healthy and unhealthy ways. Some have taken productive steps such as living more simply on purpose, limiting what's spent on entertainment, and avoiding the use of casual credit to avoid the bankruptcy they watched their parents experience. There's also a rising trend of "family days"—a kind of weekly relational Sabbath when everyone stops working in order to catch up with their Creator, family, friends, and selves.

Others have gone a step too far the other way, though, by thinking only in terms of their household's best interests at the expense of others. You can find this anywhere from the school and soccer field to the church and your youth group when parents with whom you thought you had good relationships suddenly become lawyer-like for their children's interests. One popular term to describe this development is *helicopter parenting*, as adults hover around their kids' every step (whether their kids actually need them to or not).[7]

If all of that is in motion, we may want to pay attention to how this emerging generation is responding. Several studies have shown, believe it or not, that the relationship holding the greatest influence on students is the one they have with their parents. One method to get a quick pulse of how that's translating is to pay attention to how students typically answer their cell phones when one of their parents calls them. Of course there will always be days when the reaction is negative and the parent is seen as an intrusion to whatever is happening in the moment. Over time, though, you can tell whether the young person generally sees the cell phone as a tool to stay connected with their household or as a kind of technological umbilical cord that diminishes their independence.

Many churches have been confused regarding how to respond to this trend, creating reactions that are more about retention and solicitation than deeper connections. You don't have to look hard to find church Web sites full of attractive programs for children and teenagers in the hopes that "if you hook a kid, you hook the family." In many small group ministries you find more topically driven things (based on what people vote to study) versus communally driven (based on a commitment to the group regardless of the study). You may even find church leaders who don't believe they have the freedom to lead because everyone wants to have things their way and will abandon their membership vows if they can't. If that is

---

7. This term is attributed to Foster W. Cline, M.D. and Jim Fay in *Parenting with Love and Logic: Teaching Children Responsibility.*

what's happening among the adults, how then are we to develop community among young people?

That's another really good question.

TWO PATHWAYS FOR COMMUNITY

If you had to sum up the core difference in Jesus' ministry versus the Pharisees' teachings, I believe it's that Christ was known as being "for" something while the Pharisees were known for what they felt God was "against." One might argue that this is the concept we see described when people speak of Christianity as a "relationship" versus a "religion." Certainly the Bible speaks about both, but one is intended to lead the other in individuals and churches alike.

For instance, the Sabbath was a gift God gave the Israelites after they had been enslaved in Egypt every day of the week and made this known to them through the "Tender" Commandments.[8] The Pharisees took this general guideline and created 39 categories of what might be considered "work" (e.g., walking, reaping, threshing, making a meal, lifting a burden, and so on). If someone didn't understand that list, another was made to define it—for example, how a "burden" meant anything more than two dried figs, or if a man even thought about lying down with his wife he was sinning.

Jesus came along and honored the initial gift of this Sabbath—but famously broke the man-made interpretations by healing the sick and allowing his disciples to gather food on that day of the week. (Matthew 12:1-8; John 9:13-16) When questioned by the Pharisees on this matter, Jesus responded, "The Sabbath was made for man, not man for the Sabbath" (Mark 2:27) Challenges like this left the religious leaders speechless, ultimately driving them to crucify Jesus for what they interpreted as a fundamental blasphemy against their understanding of God.

This interaction all throughout the Gospels illustrates that there is often a conflicting sense about what community is and isn't. Churches have struggled with this as well, wondering if the primary goal is separation from the world or if instead we should be a people who provide a sense of belonging. This creates two primary pathways for community to take place, and chances are you'll see one dominate your group:

---

8. I refer to the Ten Commandments in this manner because it reminds me of God's heart behind them.

WHO'S OUT?

A sense of community can be formed by being against something (or someone) for however long that object of disdain exists. For each pop-music fan who dresses in pastels, there's an alt.rock fan who dresses in black. Young people have taken on political interests as well through this venue, disagreeing about the policies and personalities of an administration in order to get a contrasting candidate elected, all through grassroots networking. Even the very concept of a clique is all about creating a culture of exclusivity in which a select group feels better about itself by looking down upon everyone else.

WHO'S IN?

Being for something and looking for ways to include others has one advantage that the other approach does not: It transcends the need to be against something and can dream of a better tomorrow on its own two feet. As Christians we don't have to search too hard to find something real beyond the norm of life that requires the devotion of our entire lives. The very nature of being the church means we're already on a mission to restore all of creation back to its Creator through responsibility, inspiration, sharing, diversity, and inclusivity. The more you help students see their lives as a part of this Grand Narrative, the more they'll be able to embrace and develop the community formed along the way.

Wisdom from the Trenches

There's a fine line between a clique and a community. A clique is closed, exclusive, and turned inward; a community is open and dynamic while still being connected. A community is family...weird uncles and all. Many youth groups tend toward becoming closed entities with their own pecking order and flavor, which, of course, works against kingdom ethics and building a family.

Some things are natural community builders: Mission trips, camps, or any project where kids are forced out of their comfort zones to work and play together. Often it takes some unpopular moves to break down the walls and build a sense of community (e.g., assigning kids who don't hang out together the same bunkhouse at a camp or busting up a too tight group for at least part of a long road trip). If you're worried this may be too much, you can do it for only part of the trip and create a "get to know you" game for kids to play while on the road.

Another sample of how this could be done in a camp or retreat setting is to give each bed or bunk a number or letter. (Give girls numbers and guys letters so you don't end up with girls bunking with guys!) Every day kids draw a new number and end up switching bunks and bunkhouses. Some kids will gripe, but if you set this up as part of the fun of camp and get your staff to cheerlead the concept, most kids will actually enjoy it.

To do this effectively you will have to explain your rationale, sell the concept, keep the mixing reasonable (after all, kids often go on mission trips and camps more because of friends than higher motives) and be fun and innovative in how it all plays out.

—*Rick Bundschuh, 37 years in youth work*

BARRIERS TO COMMUNITY

Community helps young people form identities, realize safety, and experience healing. Most teenagers understand the basic wiring God has put into us for relationships and will look for it in healthy ways when possible—or settle for it in unhealthy forms when they're frustrated. This is why youth work is ultimately about a "love God, love others" mentality that underscores what Jesus said is the most important commandment. (Mark 12:28-31) What makes it difficult, though, are the struggles inherent in most teenagers' worlds. You may see these in a few individuals or among many in your group, but each can have an overwhelming impact on the community you're developing.

POOR COMMUNICATION SKILLS

Let's face it: Life doesn't come with a scriptwriter who hands us our lines as we need them. It's difficult enough to know the perfect thing to say when you know of a situation in advance, not to mention when you're surprised by a circumstance that demands a quick response. God's gift of free will means that we all have to choose from a variety of responses to any situation, from initiating a new connection with someone we don't know to handling conflicts in our relationships.

Should we be surprised, then, when young people struggle with this issue as well? It's easy to get frustrated when we try to make a connection with them, and they merely shrug their shoulders or seem aloof at our presence. You may wonder if these teenagers even have a voice, while at the same time wishing that the ones who do would stop talking about the wrong thing at the worst possible moments. Communication is a sort of dance we're all engaged in, and students are still learning the basic moves as they step on toes and trip over their own feet.

> *Action steps:* You'll have to make the first move, and then the second move, and then the third, and possibly the fortieth, and the one hundredth, and so on. Simple yes-or-no questions can break the ice, but your goal is to find an area of passion they can start talking about with ease. Don't feel as though you have to be the expert, but instead allow them to be the authority. If you can get them talking about something that matters to them, they may just develop the chops to communicate in other ways.

ANTISOCIAL KIDS

It's not uncommon for a youth ministry to have at least one student who doesn't fit into the dominant social circle. This young person may possess a unique personality you may enjoy interacting with, but for some reason he comes across to his peers as either independent, unapproachable, impulsive, or just plain "weird." In some instances these kids manipulate the comfort others crave by lying and blaming. When they act up, others in your group may feel as if wild animals were let loose in the room to do what they pleased, and no one stepped up to intervene.

> *Action steps:* Whether or not "antisocial" kids intend to behave in antisocial ways, they matter to God and need to know that their worth is ultimately more important than their behavior. If you aren't the person to invest in them and communicate this, pray for and find someone who can effectively mentor them. There must be a voice in their lives that communicates the love of Christ through straight talk that speaks their language. If consequences ever need to take place, this individual has the credibility to either put them into place or back you up when you're the one taking action.

INCONSISTENT ATTENDANCE

This is one of my biggest pet peeves. Many kids simply won't show up on a regular basis—and end up blaming *you* for the consequences. A lot of this has to do with their busy schedules and the number of things they've committed themselves to. Others, though, will choose to not come to meetings, special events, and fundraisers simply because they don't feel like it. Either way you'll hear kids and their parents talk about how there was no connection with other students, so they decided to discontinue involvement. This can seem like the ultimate slam to all the energy and time you put into ministry, because no matter how hard you try to make the ministry appealing, someone decides that something else matters more.

Action steps: There are many related things you can't change, from sports schedules that keep kids too busy to work hours their bosses won't let them change. What you can control, though, is a flow of information that keeps students and families "in the know," even when they can't be there. Use whatever form works best for your group, whether it's through the Internet, texting, a student hotline, or physical newsletters. (There's a reason why the same root word is found in *community* and *communication*.)

HANDS-OFF MENTALITY

Our world is a global community dependent upon relationships to function. We're paid money because someone believes our skills are worth paying for; we use the paycheck from that job to buy groceries; the part-time cashier pays her college tuition because we choose to shop at that store, etc. So when students decide they won't take part in the work of your community, everyone inside and outside of it suffers. When the division of work doesn't happen, the community cannot grow as God intended it to.

Action steps: This is such a hard issue to address without coming across as manipulating or guilt-tripping students. Nonetheless you need to help them see that without their hands and feet, the body of Christ is incomplete. Set up otherwise uninterested students for short-term opportunities that provide immediate bursts of affirmation, and you may find them coming back for another bite.

OUR OWN INSECURITIES

Having led adult youth workers and been one myself, I've often found that we can at times be some of the most insecure people in the youth ministry. I've seen grown people of varying ages become blind to how they made their callings all about the desire to be needed, and I've watched others feel like failures if other small group leaders seemed more popular or attractive than they were. There were times when college-aged volunteers used the high school ministry as a place to find dates, while older adults tried to get students to help them gain the favor of other adult volunteers in whom they had romantic interests. So what's meant as a ministry to get kids to consider what God thinks of them can unfortunately become a vehicle to figure out what others think of us.

Action steps: We'll touch on this one more at the end of the chapter, but let me sum up a quick word to you on this right now: You're not alone in wondering if you're cool enough, athletic enough, artistic enough, musical enough, or smart enough to invest in students. Don't let that distract you, though, from the fact that none of that matters. You're among a great majority of ragtag people whom our God has called; not because you're exceedingly qualified, but because God can exceedingly qualify you to do your calling. And any bold-ness you feel you lack…any strength you feel you don't have…any personality change you believe you need in order to "become yourself"…is a lie.[9]

INSIDE AND OUTSIDE THE LEVELS OF ENGAGEMENT

Do your young people feel as though they matter as much as you may say they do, or do they believe they can slip out of your community without anyone noticing? That's a question you'll have to wrestle with because your group's sense of community happens both inside and outside the environments you directly oversee and serve.

Allow me to repeat that, just in case you read the words too quickly:

Your group's sense of community happens both inside and outside the environments you directly oversee and serve.

This means you'll have to develop an "inside" and "outside" approach in tension with itself in order to actively nurture community in each of these areas:

OUT-REACH: THE COMMUNITY OUTSIDE YOUR COMMUNITY

Outreach isn't about building up your weekly program's attendance; instead it's about taking the initiative to connect with young people who're disconnected from God. One way they better recognize and receive his life-changing invitation of eter-nal life occurs when you step into their world in the here and now.

Some approaches to outreach are quite unnatural and conversation-stopping. We mistakenly believe that the challenge is to win arguments and not people, but pushing others to make decisions they aren't ready for can shut down dialogue permanently.

INSIDE

The core reality of outreach to teens is that Christian youth have a responsibility to God and brilliant opportunities, so they're best placed to reach out to their peers. Helping a group of students become effective in this requires a combination of inspi-rational teaching and training, plus the provision of events to which they can invite their friends. It grows as these young members invite their nonmember friends to join the group through these platforms of invitation.

While these outreach events and programs can be useful, they are intended only as supplements to the relationships themselves. Even good techniques can't replace

---

9. See the entire chapter of Galatians 5, but specifically pay attention to verses 7-10.

genuine love, so one of the best places to start a shift for the better is through how we think, feel, act around, and pray about those we already know.

Reconsider the language we often use to define someone's spiritual condition. Calling another person a "non-Christian" may sound more permanent and pessimistic than "pre-Christians" or "seekers," for example. Offer your teens the perspective of everyone being on the same journey with God, with some ahead of others only by the experience of grace. Helping them think of their stories in connection with the story of God will better help them see how all people are made in God's image and in need of restoration back to who God declares they already are.

Help students feel the confusion of other students who're navigating life without God. When someone bothers them at school, work, home, or play, be there to hear how they feel. Take the time, though, to help these students pray for others and their disconnection from God. It's easy for us to skip over this and become so self-focused that we develop a deaf ear to others' spiritual conditions.

Build up your students' confidence and openness about their faith in how they act around others. We live in a world that's trying to impart a value of tolerance to the emerging generation. A consequence of this is that Christian teenagers sometimes feel as though everyone has the right to share their views on God except them. Afraid of becoming labeled as narrow-minded, some young people simply choose to blend in versus stand out. So allow the testimonies of others who're taking steps locally and globally to inspire them toward similar actions.

Begin praying with your teens for their friends by name. Ask your core students who they have a heart to see come into relationship with Jesus Christ, and then help them talk with God about those burdens. (You'll also want to model the value of listening, too, so ask God to speak direction into everyone's hearts about ways we can join him in reaching out.) Imagine how different your calendar might look if everyone spent a half hour doing this before you sketched out your plans for the ministry in that season.

Also, set an example for youth by asking them to pray for the people to whom you're reaching out. If they're to talk about their faith and beliefs with their friends, then they need to know and see how you do this with yours. Be honest about your struggles and contagious in your victories.

OUTSIDE

Outreach outside your ministry program isn't about providing a cool-but-watered-down expression of faith, delivering a presentation, or providing watertight answers to questions we haven't inspired others to ask. Rather it's about one human being engaging with another on that young person's territory so that teen can, in turn, engage with God. It starts with listening to the Holy Spirit and the people to whom we're speaking *before we begin to articulate why they should get together*. Accordingly that teenager will let you know when you've earned the credibility for the introduction.

Any conversations you have are dialogues and never monologues. Often you'll have to take part in frequent visits before doors are opened to discuss faith and beliefs, and even then you may find it more effective to keep visiting them before they're comfortable visiting your program. It's helpful, though, to have some things to draw on as tools to further the conversation.

A variety of opportunities: Provide intentional and credible ways for unchurched youth to feel drawn into your community. They may not normally come to a standard program or meeting, but they may feel comfortable going to a football game or messy game night you advertise locally. You may even be surprised at how many nonreligious teenagers want to join you in service projects that make immediate, tangible, lasting impacts on others. Find out what your students' friends are interested in, plan some of your events around those things, and then get the word out.

An invitation to doubt on purpose: If you find yourself speaking with teenagers who doubt some vital truths about God, dare them to explore God for a month with you and help them know that there are no strings attached. Teens often need to belong before they believe. In light of this, it isn't about ganging up on them if they do come, but being inclusive and loving believers who best demonstrate God's invitational kingdom. Providing cringe-free, relaxed opportunities to include others can help the group to experience growth from its fringes.

Be natural and help your students to do the same. Avoid pressuring your young people to approach evangelism as a sale they have to make. Pre-Christians aren't resources to be exploited so we can have another notch on our belts; they're people to be loved. So consistently encourage students to be fully faithful to the conversation of the moment, whether or not it ends with the other person taking a step of salvation.

Be everywhere that students are. Attend local plays, sporting events, musicals, and other performances to see your students and meet their friends on their own turf. Find out where kids hang out socially and look for natural ways to be there (even if it's just to provide free snacks with a card attached that has your ministry info on it).

IN-REACH: THE COMMUNITY WITHIN YOUR COMMUNITY

INSIDE

Once students walk through the front door of your youth room, they are immediately looking to take the next step. Some will want to know where they can sit and observe while others are ready and willing to jump into an activity, game, or study.

The Five-Minute Walk. In one group I served, we formed a team called "Frontline" whose sole purpose was to be sure that there was more than a quick handshake for visitors, but a lot of affirming words and significant connections. We trained our teens to give visitors a tour around our facility through a five-minute walk that broke the ice. Not only did the visitor gain a better sense of where everything was and when different things happened, but they also met a friendly face they could go to with any other questions. Whether you meet in a large building or in a house, recognize that how you handle those first five minutes can set the pace for new students' entire journeys with your ministry.

The Five-Minute Run. Another approach that inspired a healthier sense of internal community was something we called "Running Partners." The Bible uses athletic metaphors regarding how we are to run in order to "obtain the prize" to which we've been called. (1 Corinthians 9:24) Using that metaphor, on Mondays, Wednesdays, and Fridays students would check in with each other at school for at least five minutes in order to pray for each other and ask straight questions about what goals they're pursuing for Jesus that day. This proved yet another way to generate conversations and community that might've been otherwise overlooked.

OUTSIDE

There are teenagers who've recently visited, or are planning to visit, who may want to understand who you are in ways that "pop-ins" alone can't provide. Sometimes having paperwork to take home can help, as can using the time before your main all-church gatherings to showcase videos of a recent trip or promo of your ministry. Your goal is to provide more than a sense of what will happen the next time you meet but rather a true menu of opportunities so new students can feel connected, understood, and involved.

Online communities have become a popular way for teenagers to figure out their places in youth ministries and churches. They allow new students to sit in their own homes while getting snapshots of who you are and ways they might get connected. Whether it's your own Web site or a page on a social networking spot, post some of the videos and stories from previous activities you've done to inspire new teenagers looking for that next step. You may find them connecting with you online (where they feel safe) in ways they may never talk to you in person.

UP-REACH: THE COMMUNITY THAT TRANSCENDS COMMUNITY

INSIDE

There are many things that separate youth ministry from other forms of youth work, but it always comes down to our task to create environments where Jesus Christ can transform students. Along with the work of the Holy Spirit and the enduring activity of God, we get to seek and establish an influential set of conditions that provide a framework in which students can more deeply experience God. While you can never simply will community to happen, there are three ingredients you can provide:

Time. The goal here is not a certain number of quantifiable minutes and hours. Rather you're utilizing an undetermined period of time or an intentional pace to cultivate a qualitative, unanxious, peace-filled, calm, and reflective environment in which something unpredictable can occur.

Space. Any space can become sacred if it's intentionally claimed as such. You can do this by creating deliberate aesthetics that are intriguing and astonishing physically, or by simply inviting students to bow their heads and create some prayer space with God that contemplates and considers the wonder, beauty, and creativity of who God is and what God is doing.

Matter. We need to offer students something tangible to wrestle with, where it's anything from the theme of a teaching or event to a takeaway symbol that helps them better hang on to a concept. Note: The focus is never on the object itself but on the One to whom it points; the One who offers a re-created and transformed life.

OUTSIDE

Just as you can't in your own power make spiritual community happen among your Christian teens, so it's also impossible to force a non-Christian student to connect with God. You can, though, provide an authentic "up-reach" focus that's born from a collective unity to enjoy who God is and what it means to act as his body by living out his mission. Even worship music can create this type of connection, for it equalizes everyone before God and enlarges our understanding of who God is.

Make your invitations inclusive, not exclusive. Instead of salvation invitations, give opportunities for everyone to surrender to Jesus Christ. Both Christians and seekers alike find common ground at the foot of the cross.

Don't be assuming in your language. It's easy to speak of Bible stories using phrases like, "You all know the story of David and Goliath." Don't take for granted that everyone does know the stories, since those who don't will feel excluded from your study and community.

Make use of symbols. There are at least two sacraments from which teenagers inside and outside the church can gain powerful symbolism. Using the Lord's Supper (communion) and baptism does more than connect with our stories; they tell God's Story. Explain what these sacraments mean before you do them, allowing teens who are already engaged in such practices to inspire others by example to take part as well.

Allow for downer moments. Much of the Psalms speak about anger, desperation, sadness, and frustration. We often don't allow such comments or songs into our worship programs, though, for fear of becoming distracted.

Point to God outside of your meetings. It's easy to become a holy huddle that worships, prays, and studies but never follows the call of Jesus to "go and make disciples" (Matthew 28:19). May your desire to praise God never cause you to neglect going after lost sheep God's quite passionate about. (Luke 15)

CHAPTER 15

DEVELOPING STUDENT LEADERS

"Shut up and listen to me because I'm a leader!"

Something told me that my new student leadership team wasn't working out as I'd hoped.

I heard the comment come from "Dave's" mouth as he tried to get another student to move from the chair he was sitting in to a different one. That kid didn't want to move, so Dave felt it was time to pull rank.

"I said move it! You have to listen to me because I'm a W.A.K.O." (An acronym for "Willful Acts of Kindness to Others"—the irony of that statement apparently was lost on Dave.)

"Dave," I called over, "can I talk with you a minute?"

"Yeah," he said. As he came over from across the room I had the same conversation with him that many of you might have had. We talked about how leadership is about credible influence and not about a title we may wield. We covered what it means to honor Christ not just by what we say but also how we say it. We also touched base on how the goal isn't to exasperate others but to serve them in love.

Dave nodded his head and said, "Okay, I got it. I'm sorry." I encouraged him to apologize to the student he'd been arguing with. Dave agreed and went over and began his speech. "Yeah, um...so I'm sorry for telling you what to do, and I guess I'm not allowed to do that because I'm a leader." A short pause occurred. "So maybe just do it anyway, because if you don't I'll pound you."

Yes, this actually happened.

I don't share this story to fault the student but rather to illustrate my own short-sightedness in developing student leaders. Thankfully no one got pounded that night other than me...and I got it from the Holy Spirit. I'm quite sure I still have the bruises, too, all these years later.

Wisdom from the Trenches

We need to be really careful how we define *student leaders*. In some places that simply refers to the group of kids who plan special events or activities. Maybe they're the greeters at the door or help set up and tear down before and after programs. On one hand that demonstrates a certain level of leadership and certainly is the kind of servant spirit we want to see in a leader; but on the other hand it seems like a dangerous trap to give these kids a list of tasks to do and not really give them any kind of spiritual leadership role.

To me, that's all stuff we can pass off to the adults. I'm not against students doing those things, but the real key in student leadership is empowering them as spiritual leaders in their churches and student ministries. Whenever possible, it should be kids leading the prayers, the worship, the small groups, the service projects. We foster that by setting them up for success, talking them through these different ministry opportunities, encouraging them, building them up, and celebrating it whenever we see it. It takes a lot more time and work than just doing it ourselves, but if we're not equipping others for ministry, then we're missing the point.

I guess this all comes out of my time as a ministry leader in college. I'll never forget noticing year after year the incoming freshmen who initiated Bible study groups, joined campus ministries, sought out churches to attend, started worship events, and more. These freshmen all had one thing in common: They'd been empowered to be spiritual leaders in their youth groups. They had been "doing" ministry for years, and for them it was a natural thing to continue their leadership in the body of Christ wherever they went.

—*Matthew McNutt, 10 years in youth work*

SO...WHAT'S YOUR POINT?

Many voices in youth ministry believe that it's natural and necessary to involve teens in leadership, but do you? And if you do, is it because they've told you it's natural and necessary, or is it because you see the value yourself? How you answer that will determine whether you throw kids into positions of convenience or develop student leaders who are in the right places doing the right things in the right ways.

There are usually two distractions that cause us to put kids into positions for the wrong reasons:

It's "nice" to see kids doing ministry. Parents and church leaders like it when we get young people doing things that seem beyond their years, and so often there will be positive pressure to put kids in front. You may even enjoy seeing this yourself because it can feel affirming to watch kids sharing what you've been teaching them. Be careful, though, to not let the desire for something nice cause you to put kids into situations they aren't ready for.

We all need extra time to accomplish other things. You have a lot to do and probably dream about handing off all your tasks to others who could do them instead. Maybe you need a team of "roadies" to set up chairs, tables, screens, projectors, sound equipment, and so on. A group of "admins" could be sure that attendance sheets, guest cards, Bibles, and birthday cards don't get overlooked. You may even have a crew of "microphoners" who enjoy praying, leading games, doing skits, sharing lessons, or singing as part of a praise team. Would you be asking these young people to step up in order to use their gifts? Or are you looking to lighten your load? Both are important, but which is driving you?

The point of involving youth in ministry is perhaps best summed up in this verse:

> Don't let anyone look down on you because you are young, but set an example for the believers in speech, in conduct, in love, in faith and in purity.

(1 Timothy 4:12)

If we don't develop students to lead, we prevent a great portion of this Scripture from being fulfilled. Their service can create a greater dose of enthusiasm among the entire church and other teenagers in your ministry because they have their hands around a significant piece of responsibility. Voluntary participation is concerned as much with the quality of young people's involvement in activities and decision making as with their freedom to attend or not. Likewise, empowerment seeks opportunities for young people to not only bless the group but also take on a self-feeding component to their own spirituality.

Both of these values serve as reminders that young people must be involved in the group decision making and planning. Small youth groups may be able to achieve this through informal discussions involving all members, while larger groups may need to consider adopting more formal mechanisms (e.g., youth councils, ministry teams, etc.). Sometimes even deciding how decisions are made can be as significant as any other activity, helping them to develop leadership skills to be used in every other arena of life.

Again, there are many reasons to develop student leaders, and such a list can be endless and exhaustive. The goal in considering it isn't to make you start quickly handing out assignments, but rather to make you ask what your point is in involving youth in ministry. Is it all about the things that need to get done today or more about the adults you're forming for tomorrow?

THE MAKING OF A LEADER

If you've ever baked a frozen pizza, you know that there's an ideal temperature and length of time prescribed to offer you the best blend of crust and toppings. For instance, the box may instruct you to bake the pizza at 400 degrees for 20 minutes, which means someone determined this was the best way to generate the intended taste and texture. As a teenager I once tried to beat the system by turning the heat up to its highest level, assuming it would cut my time in half. You probably know the foolishness of this thinking and can imagine the number of smoke alarms I set off.

Sadly, we may take this same approach with teenagers and throw them into hot environments that only end up burning them. To avoid doing so we need to select which process we'll use to identify potential student leaders. Any of the following approaches can have merit if you consider an insight from 1 Samuel 16:7 that "People looks at the outward appearance, but the LORD looks at the heart."

YOU SELECT THE STUDENT LEADERS

Many youth workers believe in selecting students themselves, recruiting who they believe possesses the character and competence to serve within the ministry.

Pros: If you're hand selecting students, chances are you believe they have "the right stuff" to take on whatever role you ask of them.

Cons: You may be setting yourself up to ask the wrong kids while missing some good prospects God can use.

THE STUDENTS ARE NOMINATED BY THEIR PEERS

Some ministries operate by having students recommend each other to the youth council or leadership positions.

Pros: Since you can't see your students at school and others can, student nominations may provide a more comprehensive perspective regarding who's living out their faith.

Cons: This process can echo a popularity contest rather than the prayerful discernment of a community we find in the Bible.

STUDENTS APPLY FOR THE OPPORTUNITY

Many youth groups opt to have teenagers submit applications for student leadership. Using a filtering system of objective criteria as well as personal interviews, many youth workers enjoy the opportunity this affords to hear students' hearts.

Pros: This process can help screen out students who shouldn't be leaders through the standards you put in place that measure what is required for them to take part.

Cons: Some of your potentially best student leaders might see applications as busywork and choose not to engage in the process.

STUDENTS PROVE THEIR CREDIBILITY OVER TIME

A more hands-off approach is to state that after a series of tasks or an appropriate length of time, anyone can be a part of a leadership team.

Pros: There's a sense that the students have earned their place versus merely interviewed well for it.

Cons: You may feel obligated to grant teens roles that they've earned but still aren't ready for.

No one likes telling students they aren't ready for something they believe they are, but you'll do them and your ministry a disservice if you can't say no. You'll want to consider their ability to clearly identify their faith in Christ and how they came to trust their lives to him. Likewise take into account the dominant relationships with their families and friends, as well as the general vibe you get from each. While that shouldn't be a factor, it's worth noting if they will become people of many companions who will come to ruin (Proverbs 18:24).

CULTIVATING THE STRUCTURE

Once you've identified who your leadership team will be, you have to begin wrestling with the means by which you'll develop them. For example, you can begin by motivating them through extrinsic rewards (i.e. "Whoever brings the most friends this week gets a free pizza party!") or intrinsic insights (i.e. "What's the greatest thing you think God can do and wants to do in this ministry?"). Helping them link with adult Christian mentors with whom they regularly meet can also be an effective stimulus.

Next you'll need to consider the structure and values by which all things occur. Failure will happen, therefore make plans to build a culture in which it's okay to struggle forward as we serve God. Develop independent thinking that helps them feel a greater confidence and ownership in every area by giving encouragement, being enthusiastic, and showing unconditional love. This is also a great time to digest verses on biblical leadership, so utilize Titus 1:7-9, 1 Timothy 3:8-13, 1 Corinthians 13:4-8, and 2 Peter 1:5-8. As you do so together, create a running list of what your leadership structure will look like.

Establishing this structure isn't just limited to program areas. Talk about the value of relational loyalty that every ministry needs to stay healthy. This helps students become problem solvers who turn disagreements into dialogues and skepticism into trust. You gain incredible credibility with new students when another who already knows you speaks on your behalf to them. A simple, "Yeah, he's/she's cool," goes a longer way than we realize.

The bottom line is that leadership costs *something*—mainly time, availability, and a lot of hard work. Teenagers shouldn't serve just to receive praise but simply for the sake of serving. There's great joy when God is using us in our areas of strength, so help student leaders discover their gifts and strengths so they can use them in your ministry. Just make sure that you don't mix up who is more inclined to work behind the scenes and who does better up front.

Regular leadership meetings and special weekend events can allow for training to occur on a consistent basis. Not only can you lay out the groundwork for the whole year, but also you can provide refreshment and challenge for anyone involved with your endeavor. Whether you grab a book to read together or use every experience as a teachable moment, allow God to speak into this matter from every possible angle.

The other thing to take into account is that simply spending time with young people means a lot to them, especially when it happens in everyday places and ways. Allow God to speak through your life as you do the commonplace things, explaining why you're doing what you're doing and the values behind it (e.g., "I'm going to run some errands for my wife because she's busy, and I love her. Want to join me?"). The more comfortable you feel about sharing these slices of your non-ministry life, the more comfortable the students may feel within their ministry roles.

PUTTING THINGS INTO MOTION

The "W.A.K.O" leadership team was surprised when they came to their first summer meeting, and I handed them all trash bags and plastic gloves. "What are these for?" Dave asked.

"We're going to pick up the trash in the neighborhood," I answered.

"That's gross," said a junior high girl. "Why would we do that?"

"Because Jesus said that a leader is one who serves," I replied. "And if we're going to reach the students in this city who are far from God, then we need to be used to getting our hands dirty."

The students bit their lips the rest of that meeting, and when they came back, we debriefed. The next week I greeted them with the same offering of supplies.

"What? We're doing it again?" asked a student.

"Yep," I said. "We're doing it every week." I was the first to put on the gloves and head out the door. "Follow me."

Over time the numbers in our leadership team began to drop for all the reasons I hoped they would. Once you start holding students accountable to the vision, they'll either rise to the occasion and become the servant-leaders you hope they can be or decide it's not worth it. You stand a better chance at inspiring them when you set the pace, allowing yourself to embrace the very values you hope they'll take on.

The odds are against you, though, since every generation faces two competing temptations—to either live life measured by comfort and personal gratification or by selfless love and sacrifice. Tragically, even Christians are seduced by this hollow lifestyle in their desire to be "great for God." The main thrust of any leadership team is to see God so they might serve God. A training program, therefore, should involve four areas of focus:

SOCIAL EXPECTATIONS

The student leadership program itself should be a model that includes a commitment of time to meet together. You need to decide what consequences are appropriate for missing these gatherings, but there must be some effect, even a minimal one. Otherwise young people may believe that their presence really doesn't matter or impact the overall unity and preparation of the group. In this way the team itself helps serve as a reminder of the internal values that must permeate each student leader's heart.

SPIRITUAL TRAINING

It's one thing to discuss theology in church services and quite another to talk about it in everyday situations. Students must have a spiritual foundation of their own to stand on, or else they'll "leave Jesus at the building." Sometimes they'll feel a greater freedom to ask questions in the environment of a leadership team because they don't believe it'll cause other students to stumble in their faith.

SMART BRAINSTORMING

Make space for your teens to consider any issues facing your region or ministry and what role they might play in helping God with them. Let them roam free and creatively, but keep things "smart" by always propping up the big-picture mission before them. You may be surprised not only by what they come up with, but also by the way they deal with such predicaments as individuals and as a group.

STRETCHY CHALLENGES

Student leadership is not a hit-and-run relationship during youth meetings but is a means by which to draw near to needs wherever they're found. That means part of your goal is to send teenagers home to serve their parents and siblings in the same way (if not better than) they serve your group.

KEEPING IT GOING...AND GOING...AND GOING

Once in a while you'll connect with students whom you sense really have the potential to impact the kingdom of God in significant ways. Perhaps that's true of every young person, but some seem to leak it in everything they do. They're somehow more tuned into the things that the Holy Spirit is doing in their lives and in the lives around them, causing you to wonder if you should do anything different with these particular teenagers.

Within reason, you may find it helpful to expose such emerging leaders to environments and situations normally geared for adults. They may gain a tremendous amount of insight from youth ministry conferences if you were to invite them along, so be on the lookout for some that are appropriate. Likewise help these students see how they can ask questions every day of the week that help them see God within their "To Do" lists.

The other component to consider is the matter of accountability. If students believe they'll be penalized for making bad choices or deliberately sinning, they may not come to you out of fear of losing their leadership positions. Assure them that you are for them and not against them so they can know that you'll help them take the healthiest action steps that lead to reconciliation and restoration.

I won't lie to you; I've seen all of this completely backfire time and time again as students turned a very healthy leadership structure into nothing more than an extracurricular or clique they used to look down upon others. Yet I've also watched what happens when teenagers embraced opportunities and went on to become young adults who brought change to their college campuses and beyond. Pray for this—pray for it often, both publicly and privately. And if you can find a way to tell an anonymous-but-true story about two college students—one who failed, and one who didn't—use it to inspire in all the right ways.

CHAPTER 16

DEVELOPING TRANSFORMATIVE ENVIRONMENTS

Essential to any youth ministry is the environment in which youth workers nurture to most effectively guide teens into growing relationships with Jesus Christ. Nurturing transformative environments is an art. It requires intentional and strategic thinking, but most importantly it requires sensitivity to the work of the Holy Spirit. It's critical that youth workers understand and commit to the truth that the Holy Spirit brings about transformation in a teen's life. Yes, there are many ways we can help create an environment in which teens can more fully embrace the intended ways of God, but the reality is that we're not the ones who produce the fruit in their lives.

I like to think of it as a crossroads or an intersection between what we do to ready a teen through our environmental awareness and care, and what the Holy Spirit will do to bring about the transformation. We are an integral part, which is why I want to spend this chapter discussing various elements of transformative environments, but ultimately, it's the work of God through the Holy Spirit that causes a teen's transformation.

The following is a list of fundamental, necessary traits for a transformative environment. This list is not exhaustive, but it's certainly a list of traits that you and I should be intentional about fostering in each of our youth ministries. (A word of advice: Adopting these traits takes time and practice. Don't let yourself become frustrated when you realize how hard it might be to stay on top of them, but do work hard to implement each of them into every aspect of your youth ministry as much as possible.)

ESSENTIAL TRAITS OF TRANSFORMATIVE ENVIRONMENTS

Environments for transformational youth ministry are:

BUILT ON A PLATFORM OF UNCONDITIONAL LOVE

This is the foremost priority of a transformative environment. Without absolute love, we have nothing. Teens need love, want love, and must be loved without conclusion. Remember that they, like us, are unfinished people—and we unfinished people will at times make mistakes, let each other down, not be truthful at all times, not sit still, not care, not project much interest, etc. The reality, however, is that all teens from all backgrounds from all walks of life need, want, and must be unconditionally loved. This doesn't mean you don't have rules or that you don't challenge them with tough love—but it had better be unconditional.

PATIENT AND FORGIVING

It makes sense that an environment committed to unconditional love would be patient and forgiving. Spiritual growth happens at a different pace and in divergent ways for different people. Often, however, adults believe teens should be "further along" or "more serious" than teens may be ready to be. People who nurture transformative environments wait patiently and hopefully know that the Spirit has been working—and will always be working—in the lives of teens.

HIGHLY RELATIONAL

Transformative environments are personal and intimate. They seek to find ways to be involved in teens' lives. This goes beyond the memorization of names and faces and takes teens into caring, trusting, and special relationships without agendas for anything other than true and deep connection.

CHAOTIC AND MESSY

Because people who nurture transformative environments understand that not every teen is on the same journey of spiritual discovery and growth, things can feel disorganized and frenzied. They can also feel uncontrollable. Many youth workers are control freaks, and this trait can drive them crazy. However, it's critical that youth workers embrace this knowing that the Holy Spirit can work through anything and in any situation. This does not mean that your ministry doesn't need order and control; it does mean, however, that it isn't always going to feel like things are under control.

ENCOURAGING AND EMPOWERING

Building up teens with encouraging words and deeds is essential. Teens seek approval from everyone. When they receive encouragement from unlikely places (read: adults), it helps them grow more firmly into their identities. Part of encouraging teens means empowering them and giving them the authority to help direct the entire group. When I was youth pastor at a church in New York, we had a very difficult teen. I never really was able to deeply connect with this teen until one day at a retreat; the buses were waiting to take us back to our homes, and we were running late on cleaning the conference center. I took this teen aside and said, "Okay. You are in charge. I'd like for you to oversee this center getting cleaned up—every room more clean than when we moved in. And we need it done in 20 minutes." This teen looked at me with complete surprise and said, "I'm on it." He began using his leadership skills, and before anyone knew it, he made—in 20 minutes—that conference center spotless. Later that afternoon I overheard him telling his parents, "It was a good weekend; I was in charge of some of it." This teen came back with enthusiasm to every event or gathering we hosted until he graduated. He went to a local college and became one of our leaders.

One small moment of trust, of empowerment, changed his life.

DEPENDENT ON PRAYER

Do you pray for your teens? I mean, do you *really* seek the face of God on their behalf? And do you seek the face of God for the direction and success of your ministry? People who nurture transformative environments seek God regularly knowing that God is a God who hears prayers and acts on them. Prayer also humbles us. It has a way of helping us realize who's really at the helm. When was the last time you fell down on your knees, raised your hands to heaven, and said, "You are God. I am not." Prayer also keeps us in tune with what God has for the overall direction of our ministries. Prayer—both for individuals and for movements—strengthens our trust and hopes and provides a transformative culture to emerge and sustain.

DESIGNED FOR LEARNING

Transformation requires learning and the ability to grow in one's thinking. As the old saying goes, there are things we know, things we don't know, and things we don't know we don't know. Transformative environments seek to find ways to help teens embrace inquiry-based learning or the desire to seek new ideas about God, faith, and life on their own. We've discussed the importance of learning environments in previous chapters so we don't need to spend a lot of time on it here except to ask the question, "Are we designing and nurturing an environment that produces life-long learners or short-term experts?

MISSIONALLY MINDED

The mission of God must be the priority of every youth ministry seeking to cultivate and sustain transformation in the lives of teens. The mission of God to restore the world to its intended wholeness, and our helping teens engage in that mission is what youth ministry, in part, is all about.

COMMITTED TO THE ENTIRE BIBLICAL NARRATIVE

It is my experience that transformative youth ministries have a deep commitment to providing context and meaning to the entire biblical story rather than teaching propositionally. There is nothing wrong with propositions, unless we stop at them. People who nurture transformative environments find meaningful ways to help teens engage in the practice of biblical reading and reflection.

CONNECTED TO THE WHOLE CHURCH

Just as it is important to commit to the entire narrative of God, it is equally important to commit to the entire faith community or congregation. Youth ministries that seek to build a transformative culture find ways to connect what they are doing to the whole body of believers making sure that teens understand the importance of a fuller sense of community formation.

ENGAGES THE ENTIRE FAMILY

Typically we think of youth ministry as ministry to adolescents—and it is; but it's also ministry to teens' families. If the teens' families are not healthy and vibrant, then the chance of transformation occurring is limited. No one's life is truly transformed in isolation of the other "compartments" of one's life. This is why it is extremely important for us to find ways to partner with parents and other adult influences.

Transformative environments do not make themselves. It is very important to the Christian formation process of each and every teen that we work hard to find ways to create transforming opportunities that are in participation with the mission of God and under the guidance of the Holy Spirit. The things we do don't transform us, the Holy Spirit does. It is our privilege and responsibility to be aware of the divine and human intersections in our teens' lives.

EPILOGUE

The last words of a book are always the hardest to write. What can you say that you haven't already said? What is the most important idea or practice that should be highlighted? What haven't you said that you ought to say? What can you say to inspire the reader? These are the questions that go through one's head and heart. I've decided for this final word that I'll leave you with 10 statements that will hopefully cause you to think more deeply…or pick up another book to learn more…or evaluate your life and ministry…or affirm that what you are doing is worth it.

And it is.

So please take time to think on these things.

10 PROVOCATIVE STATEMENTS FOR FURTHER THINKING, CONVERSATION, STUDY, OR REFLECTION

1. Effective youth workers have the ability to draw out of teens what they bring into the relationship instead of merely replacing their identities with others'.
2. Effective youth workers show from their own lives where God is at work by providing personal examples and stories of transformation.
3. Effective youth workers see the importance of helping students with the development of their "meta-cognition"—or the ability to "think about thinking."
4. Effective youth workers embed the very truths they teach into their everyday lives. If they don't, they shouldn't attempt to teach them with any sense of authority—discovery maybe, but not authority.
5. Effective youth workers have a hermeneutic that guides their ability to help

teens navigate theological truths of the Bible with everyday life. One herme-neutical framework is to lean every decision up against Scripture, Reason, Tradition, and Experience (what Wesleyans call the Quadrilateral).

6. Effective youth workers are consistently humbled through the art of evalua-tion by self and others.
7. Effective youth workers desire ministry impact and find organic ways in which to measure it—but they're never solely led by the numbers of students in groups.
8. Effective youth workers can define the gospel by word and deed.
9. Effective youth workers understand the importance of the entire faith com-munity's responsibility to nurture transformative environments.
10. Effective youth workers have the ability to personalize theological truths in the lives of teens through the realization that all teens are different and all teens may need to bump up against the truths of God in different ways.

Find a group of youth workers either in your church or community or both and talk about these 10 statements above. Wrestle with them and make the effort to process them through the lens or context of your everyday life and ministry.

I hope that the next time you or another volunteer asks the question, "What did I sign up for?" you'll recall and reflect back on this book (and the DVD that accom-panies it) for inspiration, encouragement, and hope.

May you realize God's presence around you and yield to the guidance of the Holy Spirit as you seek to guide teens into Christian formation for the mission of God.

Share Your Thoughts

With the Author: Your comments will be forwarded to the author when you send them to *zauthor@zondervan.com*.

With Zondervan: Submit your review of this book by writing to *zreview@zondervan.com*.

Free Online Resources at
www.zondervan.com

Zondervan AuthorTracker: Be notified whenever your favorite authors publish new books, go on tour, or post an update about what's happening in their lives at www.zondervan.com/authortracker.

Daily Bible Verses and Devotions: Enrich your life with daily Bible verses or devotions that help you start every morning focused on God. Visit www.zondervan.com/newsletters.

Free Email Publications: Sign up for newsletters on Christian living, academic resources, church ministry, fiction, children's resources, and more. Visit www.zondervan.com/newsletters.

Zondervan Bible Search: Find and compare Bible passages in a variety of translations at www.zondervanbiblesearch.com.

Other Benefits: Register yourself to receive online benefits like coupons and special offers, or to participate in research.

ZONDERVAN®

ZONDERVAN.com/
AUTHORTRACKER
follow your favorite authors